"*When I Get Married* is for women of all ages and in all stages of marriage. In her thoughtful, practical, heart-wrenching, heartwarming style, Jerusha Clark demystifies our expectations of marriage and invites us into reality. It is not a harsh reality but one filled with hope and expectation. Chapter by chapter, I found myself being drawn deeper into love—for my husband, Don, and for my Savior, the truest Lover of all."

— JAN FRANK, MFT, coauthor of *Unclaimed Baggage* and
Door of Hope

WHEN I GET
Married...

Surrendering the Fantasy
Embracing the Reality

JERUSHA CLARK

NAVPRESS

NavPress is the publishing ministry of The Navigators, an international Christian organization and leader in personal spiritual development. NavPress is committed to helping people grow spiritually and enjoy lives of meaning and hope through personal and group resources that are biblically rooted, culturally relevant, and highly practical.

For a free catalog go to www.NavPress.com
or call 1.800.366.7788 in the United States or 1.800.839.4769 in Canada.

ISBN: 978-1-60006-056-4

Cover design by The DesignWorks Group | Tim Green
Cover image by Getty Images | Stuart McClymont

Some of the anecdotal illustrations in this book are true to life and are included with the permission of the persons involved. All other illustrations are composites of real situations, and any resemblance to people living or dead is coincidental.

"That's What the Lonely Is For" by David Wilcox © 1994 Irving Music, Inc., Midnight Ocean Bonfire Music. All rights administered by Irving Music, Inc. (BMI). Used by permission. All rights reserved.

Unless otherwise identified, all Scripture quotations in this publication are taken from *THE MESSAGE* (MSG). Copyright © 1993, 1994, 1995, 1996, 2000, 2001, 2002. Used by permission of NavPress Publishing Group. Other versions used include: the *Holy Bible*, New Living Translation (NLT), copyright © 1996. Used by permission of Tyndale House Publishers, Inc., Wheaton, Illinois 60189. All rights reserved; the New American Standard Bible® (NASB), Copyright © 1960, 1962, 1963, 1968, 1971, 1972, 1973, 1975, 1977, 1995 by The Lockman Foundation. Used by permission; the *Holy Bible, New International Version*® (NIV®), Copyright © 1973, 1978, 1984 by International Bible Society, used by permission of Zondervan, all rights reserved; *The Living Bible* (TLB), copyright © 1971, used by permission of Tyndale House Publishers, Inc., Wheaton, IL 60189, all rights reserved; the New Revised Standard Version (NRSV), copyright © 1989, by the Division of Christian Education of the National Council of the Churches of Christ in the USA, used by permission, all rights reserved; *The New Testament in Modern English* (PH), J. B. Phillips Translator, © J. B. Phillips 1958, 1960, 1972, used by permission of Macmillan Publishing Company; *The Holy Bible, New Century Version* (NCV) copyright © 1987, 1988, 1991 by Word Publishing, Dallas, Texas 75039. Used by permission; the Good News Translation (GNT) — Second Edition, Copyright 1992 by American Bible Society. Used by Permission; and the King James Version (KJV).

Library of Congress Cataloging-in-Publication Data

Clark, Jerusha.
  When I get married-- : surrendering the fantasy, embracing the reality / Jerusha Clark.
    p. cm.
  Includes bibliographical references (p.   ).
  ISBN 978-1-60006-056-4
  1. Marriage--Religious aspects--Christianity. I. Title.
  BV835.C877 2009
  248.4--dc22

2008036115

Printed in the United States of America

1 2 3 4 5 6 7 8 / 13 12 11 10 09

This book is dedicated to

Tom and Penny Anderson

for the countless hours you've spent

serving the Lord——

instructing singles in premarital classes,

discipling couples through marriage mentoring,

and, most importantly,

loving one another for all the world to see.

Words cannot express what you've done for our family.

Thank you.

Contents

Foreword

Jerusha Clark calls marriage a journey. Like most journeys, there are high peaks and low valleys, joy above anything imagined and low times you never wanted to experience. The journeys I like to go on the most are the ones with adventure. Marriage is an adventure, to say the least. Jerusha is about to guide you on a journey that will strengthen your marriage (or future marriage) and establish a more solid foundation. She gives no promises for a perfect marriage. In fact, you should doubt anyone who says he or she has a perfect marriage! Jerusha will help you see what a successful marriage looks like, and she will give you hope as well. You will be reminded that when a sinner marries another sinner it can get messy, but it can also be one of the most fulfilling experiences of our lifetime.

I have been married to my college sweetheart, Cathy, for more than thirty years. When we speak and write on the subject of marriage, we say that we have a "high-maintenance relationship." If it wasn't for

God's presence and perseverance, I wonder if we would have stayed married. We have had to learn to focus on the simple acts of kindness and discipline that make the journey of marriage a safe, healthy, and God-honoring one.

As you read this book, I know you will agree with me that Jerusha is an incredibly gifted writer and thinker. And in her collection of quotes in this manuscript are some of the most inspiring words on marriage and preparation for marriage I have ever read. Here is part of what I took away from reading this well-crafted book.

1. When it comes to marriage, your circumstance may not be able to change, but your attitude can change—and that makes all the difference in the world. You can't change your spouse; you can't control when marriage might happen for you. You can change your own life. As you do that, your relationships will get stronger. It just takes one person, and that person must be you.

2. You are not called to face singleness or marriage alone. Developing replenishing relationships will make you a better spouse, parent, and more genuine person. Don't try to navigate marriage or singleness on your own; it won't work.

3. God cares. The shortest verse in the Bible is "Jesus wept" (John 11:35). Jesus was moved with emotion at the death of a friend; clearly He cares deeply for relationships, and that includes your marriage. He wants the foundation of your marriage—present or future—to rest upon Him. At the end of the Sermon on the Mount, Jesus said, "Therefore everyone who hears these words of mine and puts them into practice is like a wise man who builds his house on the rock. The rain came down, the streams rose, and the winds blew and beat against the house; yet it did not fall, because

it had its foundation on the rock" (Matthew 7:24-25, NIV). Jesus went on to say that if you build your foundation on the sand, when the rain and storms of life come your way, your home will crash due to a poor foundation. Tough times come to all relationships; in this book you will be reminded that God is the creator and the sustainer of marriage. Any good journey is filled with adventure, but when it comes to marriage, you need enough preparation and foresight to have a great experience. If you're single, this book will guide you in proper thinking about marriage.

No matter where you are in your life—whether single or married—you will benefit from this book. I can't think of a more authentic person than Jerusha to guide you on this journey.

Jim Burns, PhD
President, HomeWord
Author of *Creating an Intimate Marriage*, *Confident Parenting*, and *Teaching Your Children Healthy Sexuality*

Acknowledgments

WITHOUT THE GENEROUS AND skilled cooperation of many, this book simply would not exist. I offer humble thanks to . . .

- My Creator God, my Strength and Shield—You never let me down. Thank You for walking with me every step of the way. It's all for You.
- Jeramy Clark, my wonderful husband, for standing by my side, encouraging and enabling me. I'm forever grateful that God chose *you* to hold me—in good times and bad.
- My parents, J. A. C. and LeAnn Redford, whose marriage is an incredible testimony to God's grace and power.
- My in-laws, Spence and Rona Clark. Over forty years of marriage, and still in love! Your example continually inspires me.
- My Nan, who's been a loving support and great "fan" ever since I started writing (for that matter, since I started life!).

- Louie and Louise Moesta for sharing your time, expertise, prayers, and love with me. I miss you so much.
- Kathy Hansen, my passionate, dream-big, gift-from-God friend.
- Kathy Moratto. I count it a privilege to journey through life with you.
- Lorraine Pintus for endless encouragement and godly wisdom, always given at just the right time.
- Cameron Germann. You're the *real deal,* beloved friend, and I'm honored to know you.
- Betsy Yphantides, who not only vulnerably shared her story but also read drafts and offered her thoughts.
- Rebekah Guzman for simultaneously encouraging and stretching me. I cherish our partnership on His behalf.
- Mary Lockrem, my part-time publicist! Your friendship blesses me tremendously.
- Tia Stauffer, a most excellent and thorough copyeditor.
- Jenni Key, who speaks truth into my life and the lives of many others.
- The staff at Rancho Bernardo Baptist Preschool — Kristin, Nancy, Sandy, Betty, Carolyn, Tina, Mary Ann, Becky, Stacy, Linda, Monica, and Lorena. Thank you for caring for my girls, sharing your space with me, and making me feel like part of your family.

Introduction

NOT LONG AFTER JERAMY and I got married, I began to wonder if my "happily ever after" had been waylaid at the customs desk of Chicago's O'Hare airport.

After all, the feds did ask me to declare everything I was bringing into the country. Perhaps an uncommonly shrewd customs officer noticed that I didn't report the slew of expectations and hopes, plans and dreams I carried in my newlywed heart. Some federal employee might have confiscated my fairy-tale ending . . . without me even knowing it!

Ten days before we (perhaps ill-fatedly) went through customs, Jeramy and I tied the knot in an amazing, all-I-ever-dreamed-of wedding. We honeymooned in Tortola—a virtually untouched paradise in the British Virgin Islands—and flew home to start the adventure of life together. Neither of us expected anything less than married bliss.

But somewhere between retrieving our baggage from the airport carousel and our first anniversary, it hit me: Marriage was not going to "make me happy."

The reality of this unwelcome truth was staggering, especially when I considered the facts: My new husband was a wonderful man. I genuinely loved him and felt assured of his love for me. We had fun together. We served alongside one another in church. Our parents were still married after decades together—unlike many other couples, we had personal examples of what it took to stay the course in love. And perhaps more significantly, Jeramy and I were committed Christians who wanted to honor God through our marriage. As far as I could tell, we had everything going for us.

During our first few years of marriage, Jeramy and I shared many powerful experiences—times of passionate intimacy, spiritual growth, and deep emotional understanding; silly moments of amusement; and focused times of collective work. We didn't have any of the problems we imagined would make marriage "difficult."

Why, then, was our marriage still challenging and confusing at times, problematic and painful at others?

Long before I met Jeramy, I heard that marriage—especially godly Christian marriage—was "hard work." But like one of my mentors, Jenni, recently confessed,

For some reason, I believed that simply knowing hard work would be involved should mitigate (or altogether eliminate) my need to actually do that work. I mistakenly thought that merely by acknowledging the reality that marriage wouldn't always be easy, I could somehow render it far less complicated and demanding.

There are certainly times when marriage seems much more like play than work, the rewards far greater than the exertion. I praise God for these times! But often, the labor in building a healthy and holy marriage is *anything but* effortless and comfortable.

I wanted to write this book because, for me and countless others, one of the most difficult arenas of effort in the marital relationship proves to be the dismantling of false expectations and misguided assumptions.

For more than a decade, I've had the privilege of working with singles and young couples. Listening to and participating in conversations with nearly every woman in my sphere, I've observed this common thread: Marriage is perpetually dissected or dreamed about, celebrated or criticized. *Everyone* has an opinion about what marriage should be.

If you ask singles why they want to get married, or couples why they decided to wed, you might get answers like "I want(ed) to share my life with someone," "I want(ed) someone to love and to love me," "I don't (didn't) want to spend my life alone," or "I like(d) the security of a committed relationship."

Quietly underlying many of these responses are unspoken assumptions, such as "When I get married, I won't feel lonely anymore," "When I get married, I'll always feel loved," and "When I get married, my life will be so much better."

Additional and rarely acknowledged (or verbalized) expectations for marriage hover around the issues of money, sex, and personal security. Many women believe that getting married will end their search for significance, confidence, and stability. They implicitly hope marriage will give them a sense of completeness, desirability, financial well-being, and sexual satisfaction:

- "When I get married, I won't care what other people think about me."
- "When I get married, I won't have to worry about money."
- "When I get married, I'll finally know what I should do with my life."

- "When I get married, my sex drive won't be an issue anymore; I'll be fulfilled and happy."

Despite the fact that many Christians could *intellectually* identify thoughts like these as faulty and potentially destructive, the emotional and mental power of these lies is nonetheless enormous.

Jeramy and I had some great premarital counseling, but I never evaluated the unspoken assumptions I entertained about marriage, let alone whether they were built on the solid foundation of Christ. I think many singles and young marrieds are in a similar situation.

Over the last decade, the U.S. marriage rate has plummeted dramatically. Consequently, our nation currently has the biggest singles population in its history.[1] Because many singles are now postponing marriage (sometimes indefinitely), a large percentage of today's unmarried people are significantly older than singles in other time periods. And according to marriage experts Drs. Les and Leslie Parrott, the United States also sees more than two thousand new marriages each year dissolve before a couple's second anniversary.[2] Global trends are not much different.

Most people have heard that one out of every two marriages ends in divorce. But this statistic does not include those who feel "trapped" in their marriage or those who might categorize their relationship as "emotionally over," "unhappy," or "dead." Everyone seems to know a couple (or two, or ten) facing serious marital issues.

Why are so many singles rejecting or postponing marriage? Why are so many people — even those who profess faith in God — dismissing traditional matrimony and turning instead to alternatives such as cohabitation and nonmarried coparenting? Why are so many marriages hurting or in trouble?

One significant reason is that, like me, people everywhere — both single and married — have harbored and currently hold flawed perceptions of what marriage can or should do for them. This certainly isn't the only answer to the complex questions of marital decline and difficulty, but it *is* an important and essential one.

That's why I'd like to candidly expose some of the most prominent misconceptions about marriage. My hope is to encourage singles to think rightly about matrimony *before* they make that commitment. I also pray that I might help some married folks wade through any disappointments and misunderstandings they've struggled with in the past, are currently battling, or might face in the future.

Over the past few years I've grown to cherish The Good News Bible's rendering of Proverbs 4:23, which advises, "Be careful how you think; your life is shaped by your thoughts."

What we think about marriage matters. It matters a *great deal.* How we think shapes the very course of our lives and definitely affects how we deal with relationships. Whether you're single or have been married many years, crooked thinking about marriage will lead to heartache and bewilderment.

At first glance, some of the problems couples face appear relatively simple (or insignificant). Before I got married, I heard about the stereotypical "Who squeezes the toothpaste the right way?" fights that ensnared newlyweds. I thought Jeramy and I could avoid most of these by discussing everything we could think of and by determining ahead of time not to "sweat the small stuff." What I didn't realize is how ridiculously *huge* queries like "What is the 'perfect' temperature setting for the thermostat?" could become to me.

Many of our ideas about marriage ultimately boil down to matters of preference, tradition, and upbringing more than a "right" or "wrong" way to live. Beyond toothpaste, toilet paper, and thermostats, for instance, questions about how a husband and wife elect to celebrate holidays, who handles the family budget, and whether or not a couple chooses to live in the same town for thirty years or move regularly are usually not issues of sin versus righteousness.

But imagine with me what might happen if you expect to visit your extended family each Christmas, while your husband wants to spend time at home. Or what if you are accustomed to celebrating every holiday, anniversary, and birthday with elaborate decorations and big surprises, while your husband grew up with the impression that such things are extravagant and unnecessary—in his mind, a simple expression is the most loving kind? What if you assumed that your husband would handle the finances, but his mother always did it for their family, and he presumed you would for yours? What happens to a wife who would like to put down roots and settle into a community, while her husband would like to explore a new place every couple of years?

Though premarital counseling and marriage-building books might help couples talk through some of these matters, it's impossible to anticipate everything involved in an intimate relationship. Surprises—and probably some downright shocks—are unavoidable. Relationships expert H. Norman Wright hit the nail on the head: "Though hints of . . . differences appear in courtship, often the huge gulf does not yawn open until after marriage, when the two are thrust together for 16 hours a day, not just when they want to be together."[3] At this crossroads, best-selling authors Bill and Pam Farrel assert that virtually "every couple goes through a period where they wonder, 'What have we gotten ourselves into?'"[4]

And here's the kicker in it all: The surprises, the outrages, the differences, and even the "what have we done?!" fears might be easier to deal with if they didn't touch so inconveniently on *much deeper* issues.

When how to celebrate a holiday becomes a question of whether a spouse feels loved and valued; when who handles the money gets mixed up with questions of provision, security, and spiritual leadership; when the numbers on a thermostat stand more for the warmth or frigidity of a relationship than the interior temperature of a home — *that* is when couples start looking at each other across an ever-expanding canyon of disillusionment.

At such a point, some couples attempt to bridge the gap by solving what appear to be their problems. Perhaps they make mature compromises about celebrations, determine an equitable division of labor, and endlessly discuss the minutiae of day-to-day living. But what happens when frustrations still creep in and discontent refuses to go quietly? What if changing habits and circumstances isn't enough to stem the tide of gnawing restlessness?

I believe singles and couples will best be prepared for and successful in marriage if they look first and most intently at their basic beliefs about matrimony — the *thoughts* they regularly entertain about marriage. People can spin their wheels for years, trying to clean up their behavior and addressing surface-level issues, when what might be needed is a pervasive reordering of their minds' and hearts' expectations.

For instance, assuming that marriage would make me happy led to a host of difficulties in my relationship with Jeramy — concerns that ultimately couldn't have been solved by changing outward actions. Because what I think determines what I do and say, eventually shaping my very character, my *thoughts* needed to be transformed before altering my behavior could make any lasting difference.

In his classic work *The Marriage Builder*, Christian psychologist Dr. Larry Crabb identified "the appealing emphasis on becoming happy and fulfilled" as a major flaw in most people's view of Christian marriage (and, ultimately, of the entire Christian life).

Uppermost in the minds of many Christians, [though] perhaps unconsciously, is a preoccupation with following Christ to achieve the abundant life of pleasant, satisfying emotions and fulfilling, enriching opportunities. . . . The joy and peace available to the Christian have become confused with the similar sounding but very different idea of [personal] fulfillment.[5]

This is certainly not to say that God has anything against happiness or fulfillment in marriage. It simply raises the question of expectation to a different level: How would our thoughts about marriage change if we believed that even more than wanting to make us happy, God created marriage to make us holy?[6]

Happiness and holiness are *by no means* mutually exclusive in marriage. (We can thank God for this truth and rejoice that a healthy marriage does bring great joy!) Still, viewing marriage primarily through the lens of holiness can transform how both singles and couples deal with basic assumptions about love, family, sex, and money. Contemplating ideas like this pushed me to explore what I believed would happen—and what others believe will happen—"When I get married . . . " The result of my research has translated into the resource you now hold.

I've structured this book to apply the Bible, God's timeless Word, as well as the wisdom He's given to those who've gone before me, to ten specific and prevalent misconceptions people often entertain about marriage. At the end of each chapter, you'll also find some questions for small-group discussion or solo journaling, intended to help you press into what you're reading.[7] Whether you're single or married, I hope that together you and I can journey through these ideas, delving deeply into the hidden recesses of our minds and hearts, letting Christ shine His light there.

As we begin to rethink our basic understanding of marriage, we will perceive that if marriage is a delightful blessing, it is also a call to servanthood and refinement. If it is full of the most profound joys, it also overflows with the most painful sufferings. Through marriage, God can sanctify two imperfect people who have vowed—and continually choose to vow—an unconditional commitment to one another.

If God grants or has granted you the gift of marriage, you will inevitably taste the bitter effects of loving in a fallen, broken world. Our longing for perfect harmony and intimacy will never be satisfied this side of heaven. But we can avoid some of the grief and regrets of this life by purposefully aligning our thoughts with God's, our ways with His.

One of the ways we can do this is by noting, right at the start of our journey, that God's plan for every life does not include marriage. First Corinthians 7:7 plainly states, "God gives the gift of the single life to some, the gift of the married life to others." I don't know whether that encourages or enrages you. But I do know that whether you are currently married or single, God's design for you is good *right now*. He *will continue* to orchestrate loving plans for your future (see Jeremiah 29:11). I don't say this to simplify or trivialize the longing for marriage single readers may feel. I would never wish to do that. Wrestling with whether or not God has marriage in store for you is just not the focus of this book. My aim is to help both singles and couples think about the realities of marriage with balance, truth, and wisdom.

If this is your desire, I give you the same encouragement Paul offered his beloved Romans: "Let God transform you . . . *by changing the way you think*. Then you will know what God wants you to do, and you will know how good and pleasing and perfect his will [for marriage, and everything else] really is" (12:2, NLT, emphasis added).

With that in mind, let's venture on, allowing the Lord to reveal our misperceptions and renovate our thinking.

ONE

I'll Always Feel Loved

THE YEAR I TURNED twenty, I read Fyodor Dostoyevsky's masterwork *The Brothers Karamazov*. Actually, I devoured the book. *The Brothers K* seemed like a daunting read when I first picked it up. (Hundreds and hundreds of pages by a gone-to-glory Russian whose name is nearly impossible to pronounce correctly, let alone spell? This wasn't exactly my idea of spring-break relaxation!) But after listening to a sermon series by a teacher I deeply respected, I was convinced I needed to read this classic tale of suffering and redemption, love and loss. I was not disappointed.

The piercing wisdom of *The Brothers K* is incomparable. But one particular quote, which seared my mind even more than countless others, came early in the novel from the mouth of Dostoyevsky's brilliant character-creation Father Zossima.[1] A society woman asks Father Zossima how she might achieve immortality and presses him to analyze her distressing lack of faith, which she believes is hindering her ability to love. The woman insists she enjoys caring for others, but also wants an immediate reward for it. Upon hearing this, Father Zossima replies shrewdly yet compassionately:

> I am sorry I can say nothing more consoling to you, [but] love in action is a harsh and dreadful thing compared with love in dreams. Love in dreams is greedy for immediate action, rapidly performed and in the sight of all . . . but active love is labor and fortitude and for some people, too, perhaps, a complete science.[2]

You didn't know me at twenty, but idealistic hardly covers it. I didn't fancy myself unrealistic, but was I full of inflated dreams and impossible expectations? You bet. The illusory love of my dreams—and I'm not just talking about the romantic love that I hoped for, ached for in a physical, hurt-in-the-pit-of-my-stomach kind of way; I'm also talking about the spiritual love I sought in my Savior's arms—was warm and fuzzy. It made me feel safe, whole, and strong. At least it did in my dreams.

Yet when Jesus drew me nearer in True Love, and when I actually began to practice loving Jeramy, whom I eventually married, there was much more pain than I had bargained for, much less that was instinctual and natural about loving. There were fewer immediate rewards than I envisioned and a whole lot of labor and fortitude required.

I thought that for Christians, love was supposed to be easy; I thought it should flow organically from the center of my being. Instead, I discovered what Jesuit scholar Dean Brackley aptly noted: "What love requires is not always obvious. Above all, love demands sacrifice, and we are slow to sign up for that."[3]

I am slow to sign up for sacrifice. And surrender. And everything else that makes love really *work*. I want the passionate kisses and someone to hold me when I'm scared and tell me that he'll never leave me, but I don't usually jump to it when "I forgive you," "I'm sorry," and "Let's do it your way" are necessary.

Perhaps old Fyodor Dostoyevsky knew a thing or two about love. His words through Father Zossima don't indicate that love is always harsh and dreadful . . . and we can thank God for that! But compared to the love of our dreams—the love we often *expect* from a spouse and *assume* will be ours—true love can seem a severe and unkind reality.

To flesh this out, let me share with you how these ideas influenced my girlfriend Betsy's life. I wish you could sit down with Betsy and hear her tell this story over a cup of tea. You would love her. In fact, I don't know anyone who doesn't adore Betsy. She's a riot and a sweetheart and an incredible mother. Beautiful, too. But even for someone as strong and fabulous as Betsy, it was hard to realize that getting married didn't equal an unending supply of "perfect" love—either from or for her. I'm getting ahead of myself, though. I'll let Betsy's words communicate how God used the experience of *not* feeling loved to draw her closer to Himself . . .

He Handed Me a Bible!
As told by Betsy Yphantides

Phil and I met at church the summer after we graduated from college. We dated for a year and a half before getting engaged and then planned our wedding for a year and a half later. That meant Phil would be finishing medical school at roughly the same time we said, "I do."

Before Phil and I got married, I didn't spend a ton of time thinking about what marriage would be like. I had always heard, though, that marriage completes people, so I guess I believed that through marriage I would become spiritually and emotionally whole. I honestly don't know where I got that. But it was there in me—and big time.

I also believed that being married, I would feel loved and adored at least 99 percent of the time (nobody's perfect, right? . . . so that 1 percent could account for our "bad days"). At one point during our engagement, I remember Phil scuffed up my rose-colored glasses; he told me marriage would be tough and that though he was expecting the worst, he hoped to be pleasantly surprised. How offensive!

I got over that day's hurt, but Phil's choice commentary on our future prospects hadn't come to an end. He would say things like "Love is a decision, and I've decided to love you—even when it gets hard." He's decided? Where are his feelings? Won't we always feel love for each other? I wondered.

Honestly, I didn't appreciate his unidealistic attitude. How could he think it was going to be so hard? We got along incredibly well; we never even fought. Why would things suddenly change with a ceremony? I assured him he was wrong; I was right, and marriage would be wonderful.

There was just the tiniest little problem. Things did suddenly change with a ceremony.

Especially when we first got married, I wanted Phil to meet all my needs. It was as if the ring went on my finger and Phil went on my life pedestal. And because I had put him on mine, I wanted to be on his life pedestal, too (that seemed only fair). I wanted him to keep my love tank overflowing by putting me first in everything. When he wouldn't, I would get frustrated that he wasn't keeping my tank full. Surely his tank was full, I reasoned; he was married to me, and I was keeping him in his "rightful place"!

My disappointment, letdown, and unmet expectations nailed me between a rock and a hard place. I couldn't quite grasp how to get above or around or out of it. There were tears, frustrations, heated conversations, and confusion surrounding this love mystery.

Unfortunately, I was trying to shove Phil into that place in my heart that only God can fill. Not only was it unhealthy for me; I was also foisting terribly unrealistic expectations on my husband. I remember Phil actually placing my Bible into my hands, directing me to go to God and ask Him to meet my needs.

It worked, and we haven't had a fight since!

Okay, maybe not. But wouldn't that have been nice?

No, at first I was seriously offended; it seemed he was trying to get out of his love responsibilities to me, or worse, he was trying to act as the Holy Spirit, convicting me of sin. But the more I thought about it, the more it made sense. Slowly, I began lowering my expectations of Phil and looking to the Savior to meet my needs for love. I took Phil off the throne of my life and asked Jesus to resume His rightful place.

Now that I look back, I'm so grateful that before we got married, Phil made the decision to love me . . . with or without feelings. Now that my "cute" factor is on its downward slope [author's note: so not true!], I'm grateful my husband bases his love on a choice instead of fleeting feelings. Emotions cannot direct life; they just enhance it.

After we were married, our single friends would often ask Phil for relationship advice in front of me. He would respond with, "The key to happiness is lowered expectations." When I assumed that Phil would meet all of my needs for love and affection, security and completeness, I hated this counsel. A lowered expectation . . . is that how he saw me?

These words certainly aren't fluffy and warm, but through the years, I've found there is deep truth to them. With Phil's lowered expectations I am free to make mistakes . . . lots of mistakes. I don't have to worry about disappointing someone who is expecting disappointment. How freeing! In similarly lowering my expectations of Phil, I can allow him to be himself, without the pressure of making me happy. He can have a bad day and it's okay; I don't take it personally. A lot of joy comes from not having to make each other happy. Our dependence is taken off each other and placed on the right Person: our perfect heavenly Father, who never lets us down.

Being in Love

When *Psychology Today* asked people, "What makes a good marriage?" 90 percent of the population answered, "Being in love." No surprise there. When the article's author pressed a thousand college-aged readers to list the "essential ingredients of love as a basis for marriage," however, "no single item was mentioned by at least one half of those responding."[4] In other words, people can't seem to agree on what love is. Or perhaps, to say it more accurately, people don't actually *know* what love is.

And really, hasn't love always struck people as somewhat of a mystery? "There are three things that are too hard for me . . ." wrote the ancient sage Agur, "four I don't understand: the way an eagle flies in the sky, the way a snake slides over a rock, the way a ship sails on the sea, and the way a man and a woman fall in love" (Proverbs 30:18-19, NCV). Today, scientists can explain a good deal about these things, but even the most brilliant biologists and physicists cannot explicate love with precise terms and formulas.

When genuine love—or even the potential for love—strikes us, we're usually baffled by the accompanying physiological cues. Certainly, something different happens to us—our hearts race, our minds are blurred, our bodies respond in what seem like crazed and irresponsible ways (I remember sweating in the most ridiculously unfeminine way on first dates)—but most of the time, we can't pinpoint exactly what's going on.

Unfortunately, people often mistake these biochemical reactions (well, maybe not the sweating) for love itself. The conglomeration of physical feelings, however—from butterflies in the stomach to the anticipation before physical consummation—is merely *a portion* of what constitutes love. Regrettably, these powerful biochemical reactions can deceive and mislead well-meaning people. Hormones can make someone *feel* genuinely "in love," but again, physical feelings account for only part of authentic love.

God's gifts to us, through modern medicine and science, can help us discern better. Brain chemicals do not have to rule us. In their book

The Singlehood Phenomenon, Drs. Beverly and Thomas Rodgers help singles understand the role biochemistry may play in falling "in and out" of love. I highly recommend their exploration of this topic. For the purposes of this book, however, I'd like to focus on only a couple of brain chemicals, which specifically influence the way people view love as well as the people they love.

According to Drs. Rodgers and Rodgers, and the researchers they partnered with, extremely high levels of phenylethylamine and norepinephrine can be detected in couples who report mutual attraction or intense romantic feelings or who claim to be "in love."

Phenylethylamine (PEA for short) is a naturally occurring neurochemical and a cousin to street amphetamines. It creates a biological "high." But as with any related amphetamine, PEA can inspire an intense yet false sense of well-being.[5]

"When PEA is flowing through our bodies," the Rodgers wrote, "we tend to be unrealistically optimistic."[6] We're literally *high* on young (as in the early stages of) love. PEA can create what the Rodgers termed "attraction junkies," people who confuse brain-chemical highs with true love. They are addicted to the feelings that accompany a new relationship and may become "serial monogamists" who go from one serious relationship to the next but rarely commit to marriage.

Norepinephrine, another brain chemical associated with love in its early stages, raises blood pressure, increases excitement, exhilarates us, and gives us excessive energy. As the Rodgers observed,

> *This is what gives us our extra zip when we are getting to know a possible mate. Norepinephrine puts that spring in our step and allows us to go without sleep and food in pursuit of our loved one. This superhuman feeling [can make you] think that each relationship must be the "real deal," only to realize much later that it had been powerful neurotransmitters operating in [your] body.*[7]

Perhaps the biggest problem with both PEA and norepinephrine is that "as with most chemicals in the system, our bodies build up a tolerance to [them]. After a while it takes more and more PEA to produce love's special kick. As the chemical wanes, a more realistic image of our partner appears."[8]

PEA, in particular, seems to run a long course in the body. Drs. Rodgers and Rodgers noted,

While there are dips in one's PEA levels—first at three months, then two years—it takes about four years for PEA to run its full course. By the four-year mark, the effects of PEA and the many other brain chemicals wear off and we no longer feel love's special kick. Our partner falls off his or her pedestal and becomes a mere mortal.[9]

Okay, so I know some of that is pretty technical. But even if you have no interest in brain chemistry, think of the effect this could have on a relationship, especially one that leads to marriage. You're on a "high" for the first three months of dating, engagement, or marriage . . . so in love. But after that, perhaps there are some bumps in the road. Maybe by two years, the pedestal is starting to crack. By four years, "love's special kick" has definitely worn off, and the person you once thought you could kiss all night and into the next day . . . well, you stop making out like you used to.

What happened? Do people just "fall out of love" or come up against "irreconcilable differences" like divorce lawyers seem to think? Is our disappointment in love simply the result of brain chemicals flying around inside us? As the apostle Paul might say, "By no means!"[10] But knowing that there *is* a natural and biochemical reason why our loved ones fall from grace can help us *decide* to love rather than allow those chemicals to rule us.

Perhaps that's why the Holy Spirit inspired Paul to write these words to his beloved Philippians:

> So this is my prayer: that your love will flourish and that you will not only love much but well. Learn to love appropriately. You need to use your head and test your feelings so that your love is sincere and intelligent, not sentimental gush. Live a lover's life, circumspect and exemplary, a life Jesus will be proud of. (1:9-10)

A lot of what we hear about love is sentimental gush, when what we need is so much more than that. I want to live a lover's life, a life Jesus will be proud of. It just seems difficult sometimes to admit that the best and wisest and *right* course is through sincere and intelligent love. Those words fly in the face of our obsessed-with-spontaneity and consumed-with-passion world. Tragically, people either assume that sincerity and intelligence can't be spontaneous and passionate or dismiss sincere and intelligent love as boring, old-fashioned, and flat.

Think back to my friend Betsy and her husband, Phil. Remember his counsel to unmarried friends — the key to happiness is lowered expectations? What if, going into marriage, you expected that you were *not* going to be loved 100 percent of the time; that you *were* going to be disappointed now and then; that, in different ways and at different times, you *were* going to fall in and out of love with your spouse (meaning your feelings would ebb and flow, and though you wouldn't always *feel* loving, you could still choose love)? What if you assumed — before you got married and throughout the course of your married life — that all of this was normal and okay?

Would this, just maybe, be a sensible and intelligent way to approach marriage? Would this, just maybe, be a loving way as well, considering that you would be taking a huge weight of pressure off any spouse you might be blessed with?

Maybe this is beginning to make sense to you, but let me play devil's advocate for a moment and place before you one of the problems I faced as a single woman: I didn't *want* to fall in and out of love. Even more significantly, I didn't want my husband to fall in and out of love with me.

After I was married, I tried to wrap my brain around the idea that Jeramy and I couldn't always feel for one another what we did on our wedding day. But I wanted that passion to last. I wanted our experience to be different, our Eden to remain intact. Let's take a couple of minutes and explore what we're really looking for when longing to be loved "perfectly."

With an Everlasting Love

"One advantage of marriage," claimed popular author and speaker Judith Viorst, "is that when you fall out of love with him or he falls out of love with you, it keeps you together until you fall in again."[11] I read that in a marriage book somewhere. And I think it was supposed to be encouraging . . . you know, the commitment of marriage is more powerful than your feelings and all that. Let me assure you, I wholeheartedly believe this, and it's great, and hip, hip, hooray for commitment.

But . . . as I mentioned before, I don't *want* to fall in and out of love. I don't want Jeramy to fall in and out of love with me. It scares me. No, scratch that; it terrifies me.

When Anne Morrow wed Charles Lindbergh, I don't know what she expected from marriage. I imagine she could foresee problems (and rather big ones) from the get-go. Lindy, as her husband was known, didn't share Anne's zeal for literature and poetry. In a day when international stardom was *not* an everyday sort of thing, her husband was a superstar. She couldn't have known, but their first child would be abducted from his crib and murdered not far from their home. Anne Morrow Lindbergh carried deep sorrow in her days as a wife.

The wisdom that suffering brought her is both powerful and piercing. In her book *Gift from the Sea,* Anne Morrow Lindbergh described what I've often wrestled with in my own love (and lack thereof):

> *When you love someone you do not love them all the time, in exactly the same way, from moment to moment. It is an impossibility. It is even a lie to pretend to. And yet this is exactly what most of us demand. We have so little faith in the ebb and flow of life, of love, of relationships. We leap at the flow of the tide and resist in terror its ebb. We are afraid it will never return. We insist on permanency, on duration, on continuity; when the only continuity possible, in life as in love, is in growth, in fluidity — in freedom.*[12]

I am so afraid that if love recedes, it will never return. I don't want to fall in and out of love because I don't trust fluidity. I guess in some ways I don't really trust freedom. I suppose I'll never fully understand His kind of love—a love that expects nothing, but hopes everything.

But I want to. I really do. And I want you to get it too. I want you to walk down the aisle confident that when the love for your spouse ebbs and flows, He will bring it back. If you're already married, I want you to trust—without a shadow of doubt—that His love is strong enough to hold you during the tide and turbulence of life.

Our God is in the business of new life, beauty from ashes, hope from fear, something from nothing. "[Wherever] you send your Spirit, new life is born to replenish all the living of the earth" (Psalm 104:30, NLT). Redemption, grace, renewal . . . these are His tools. And the love He forges is the only love that really lasts. While we frantically seek permanence in the infinitely unstable, while we're busy trying to find love and peace in the eternally unsatisfying, He's beckoning. Softly and tenderly, Jesus is calling . . .

And what kind of love does He offer? Is it a love that ebbs and flows like the love of an earthly spouse? Is His a fall-in-and-out-of-love feeling? No, no, a thousand times no. And yet there are times I can scarcely believe this truth. It's so scandalously beautiful, so hopelessly rich.

"I have loved you with an everlasting love," God proclaims in Jeremiah 31:3 (NIV). You are so valuable that "you were bought at a price," He tells us in 1 Corinthians 6:20 (NIV), and it's the highest price one can pay—Life Himself. Romans 15:7 reminds us, "Christ accepted you" (NIV).

Our Savior cries out:

> *Do not fear, for I have redeemed you;*
> *I have called you by name; you are Mine!* . . .
> *You are precious in My sight* . . .
> *You are honored and I love you* . . .
> *For the mountains may be removed and the hills may shake,*
> *But My lovingkindness will not be removed from you,*
> *And My covenant of peace will not be shaken. (Isaiah 43:1,4;*
> *54:10, NASB)*

Don't skim these verses, even if you've read them many times. Go back and let the words sink into your mind and heart: *You are Mine . . . you are precious . . . you are honored . . .* and *I love you.* You are incomparably valuable, eternally cherished, and fully acceptable to the God who created you, loves you, and died so that you could spend eternity with Him. This is the love you are looking for. And no boyfriend, no spouse, no human is ever going to give this to you. You can't absorb this love from a book, a sermon, a CD, or a friend. You have to experience it for yourself.

In the original text of the Bible, several different words are used for the verb we render in English "to know." The Greek verb *gnosis* connotes an experiential knowledge, a deep connection between the knower and the thing or person known. This is the way we are urged to know God. Indeed, the picture of eternal union between Christ and His church is a husband and wife—the most intimate portrait of relationship humans can conceive of.

If people lived as if they *really believed* the verses that we've looked at in this section, if people *genuinely trusted* in their belovedness, the world would be a very different place. I need God's grace every day to live out the truth behind these words about His love, and I imagine that you need that same grace. Why do we not ask for it? "You do not have," wrote Jesus' half brother James, "because you do not ask God" (James 4:2, NIV).

As my friend Betsy has learned to do, as I am learning day by day to do, let us ask God to meet our needs for love. Let us ask Him to remind us of who we are: His beloved ones—cherished, valued, precious, and honored. And let us entrust ourselves to the permanence of His perfect love . . . forever.

The Pain of Practice

As we begin to trust more completely in the Lover of our souls and in our own belovedness, we find it easier to expect healthy and realistic things from the people we relate to and love here on earth. This helps take pressure off our relationships and establish better channels for communication, physical expression, and mutual sharing.

But even growing in understanding cannot entirely eliminate pain from love's equation. I wish that I could tell you differently. But I would be a bad guide were I to mislead you on this point. So I will tell you the truth. I'm quite sure it will not shock you, since you have likely experienced this yourself: Love hurts.

As Mike Mason so beautifully wrote in *The Mystery of Marriage*,

"Love aims at revelation, at a clarifying and defining of our true natures. It is a sort of sharpening process, a paring away of dull and lifeless exteriors so that the keen new edge of a person's true self can begin to flash and gleam."[13]

Of course, the difficulty in this statement is immediately apparent: Sharpening is an inherently painful process. Try to extract the pain from love, and you'll have nothing left. Try to escape the breaking process, I dare you. Mason called it "excruciating" and "inexorable." No one is man or woman enough to take it. And what's the worst thing about it? What breaks us is not some nebulous force "out there," but *love,* love Himself.[14] No wonder Dostoyevsky called love in practice a harsh and dreadful thing compared to the love of our dreams.

And so people begin to build up secret resentments to the demands of marriage. They start to hold back, to see what they can get away with, to give reluctantly and then only what is *absolutely necessary.*[15]

If, however, we can go into marriage knowing that our spouse will fall from grace, that we will not always feel exactly the same about him as we did on the wedding day (or the best day of our courtship), if we have settled in our minds and hearts where our value and worth come from—what makes us lovable and accepted—then we can actually face this refining, often exhausting dimension of love without fear and trepidation.

It does not unnerve me like it used to that God will (and, boy, does He ever) use Jeramy to smooth out my rough edges. He is sharpening me through relationship with Jeramy Alan Clark, and, by grace that I cannot comprehend, I get to be part of Jer's growth too. As Mason described it, we are beginning to flash and gleam, our dull edges being pared away. And let me tell you, the pain is worth it.

Love demands everything. This is one of its chief characteristics. Unless you are challenged to overhaul your character, be turned inside out and upside down (for the better, of course), you are not really in love. Loving Jeramy has made me more patient, more gracious, more forgiving, more merciful, more loving, more generous . . .

But can I confess how agonizing it was—and still often is—to see how *im*patient and *un*gracious I am deep down? How slow I am to forgive, how stingy I am with mercy and love and money? I say that I am "more" of these things, but you have no idea how far I still have to go!

Loving just one man for your whole life is probably the single most important and most humbling experience you can have on this planet. I pray that for you, though. If it happens, I pray for your courage and stamina. You will need both for the sharpening process. Indeed, without them, without *Him,* it is impossible.

If you ever get serious about love, you can make a symbolic gesture of surrendering everything, even backing it up with a dramatic (and public!) statement to that effect—which, by the way, is what happens at every wedding. But this is just the beginning. The "I now pronounce you man and wife" merely starts you on a lifelong journey of handing over absolutely everything, and not just the things you have . . . I'm talking about everything you *are*.[16]

Does this vision of marriage—or love—disappoint you? Does it seem unromantic or just too darn difficult? I genuinely hope not. I'm not writing any of these things for mere shock value or with the desire to scare people away from marriage. That couldn't be further from my desire!

Instead, I hope any disenchantment will be what nineteenth-century British author Eliza Tabor once claimed it could be: "Disappointment to a noble soul is what cold water is to burning metal; it strengthens, tempers, intensifies, but never destroys it."[17]

Let your love—True Love—be strengthened, tempered, and intensified but never destroyed. Listen to the words of God through His prophet Isaiah: "I have refined you but not in the way silver is refined. Rather, I have refined you in the furnace of suffering. I will rescue you for my sake—yes, for my own sake!" (48:10-11, NLT). Through love, He will refine you and make you more and more like Himself . . . for His own sake.

When I was going through a particularly difficult time in life, someone forwarded me an e-mail about silversmithing. Apparently, for silver to be refined, it needs to be placed in an incredibly hot furnace again and again, until all the impurities are burned out. The e-mail's author asked the silversmith working that day how he knew when the silver was finally ready. "That's easy," the smith said with a smile. "It's done when I can see my reflection in it."

God is refining us in—and with—love so that He can see His image more perfectly reflected in us. And the ironic beauty is that He does it because of love. He loves us so much that He uses love to make us more lovable.

Marriage may not always make you feel loved, but the Creator of marriage will. If you define your life in and through His love, none of the refinements of marriage, the disappointments that come, or the ebbs and flows of intimate relationship will break you. And that is a gift beyond price.

Pressing On . . .

1. How does the idea that love might require "labor and fortitude" (work and strength) strike you with fear? Intimidation? A loud *Amen!*? What in our modern Western society makes us afraid of diligent labor? Why do you think most people would like to disassociate love and work?

2. In their book *Saving Your Marriage Before It Starts,* Drs. Les and Leslie Parrott noted,

> *Each of us constructs an idealized image of the person we marry. The image is planted by our partner's eager efforts to put his best foot forward, but it takes root in the rich soil of our romantic fantasies. We want to see our partner at his best. We imagine, for example, that he would never become irritable or put on excess weight.*[18]

Why is it important to evaluate realistically our own romantic fantasies (or, as Dostoyevsky called it, "the love of our dreams")? Ask the Lord to help you confront any lingering falsehoods or illusions about what being in love, being married in general, or being married to a specific person might be like. What did you discover as you journeyed in prayer with the Holy Spirit?

3. At many weddings, the pastor will read from the famous "love passage":

> *Love is patient and kind. Love is not jealous or boastful or proud or rude. Love does not demand its own way. Love is not irritable, and it keeps no record of when it has been wronged. It is never glad about injustice but rejoices whenever the truth wins out. Love never gives up, never loses faith, is always hopeful, and endures through every circumstance. Love will last forever. (1 Corinthians 13:4-8, NLT)*

The older I get, and the more I've tried to love, I'm often struck with the sheer impossibility of these words. No human can love in this way. Our only hope lies in aligning ourselves with the One who *is* Love, the One who can pour love through us and on us. Spend some time discussing or journaling about your need for *His* love and *His* help in loving others.

4. Have you ever struggled to believe that God loves you with an ever-lasting love, no matter what you've done? Consider this truth: God *never* conditions His love for you on your behavior. What does that statement mean to you? Is it difficult for you to grab hold of that truth and live out of it on a daily basis? How might your life be different if you lived in consistent and confident assurance of His love?

5. During a particularly rebellious period in Israel's history, God lamented over His children: "The bellows blow fiercely. The refining fire grows hotter. But it will never purify and cleanse them because there is no purity in them to refine" (Jeremiah 6:29, NLT). When it comes to your own refinement, what materials are you giving God to work with? Do you fill your life with goodness, truth, and beauty that there might be "purity in [you] to refine"? None of us seeks righteousness perfectly, but regularly filling our lives with moral filth and toxic thoughts will make it even more difficult for the Spirit of God to refine us, whether through marriage or some other means. What commitment regarding your purity and His refinement would you like to make to the Lord?

TWO

I'll Feel Whole, Complete, and Satisfied

IN THE LAST CHAPTER, my girlfriend Betsy described her expectation that marriage would make her feel perpetually loved, cherished, and valued. Betsy also confessed, "I had always heard . . . that marriage completes people, so I guess I believed that through marriage I would become spiritually and emotionally whole."

Because the two — very complex — assumptions Betsy's story revealed were bigger than one chapter could handle, I decided to focus the last chapter on whether marriage can make us feel loved and worthy of love. With this chapter, I will explore the closely related question of whether marriage completes us.

It's a rather complicated and somewhat tricky matter, this business of being completed by and in marriage. And as with many of the expectations we'll tackle together, there is some truth in the idea: God can, indeed, use marriage to help make a person whole. The keys to that statement, however, lie in the "*God* can" and "to *help*."

By itself, marriage cannot make you complete, nor will it perfectly satisfy you. The broken parts of your heart—and each of us has them—will not be healed by marriage alone. But just as God can use marriage to express love to us, allow us to experience the value He's given us, and compel us to seek Him as the source of love, He also makes use of marriage in the restoring, healing, and completing processes of life, all of which *He* authors and perfects (see Hebrews 12:2). Christ, and He alone, can make you complete, whole, and satisfied.

In the late 1990s, a wildly popular film culminated with the words "You complete me." For many young people, this served as a defining phrase for their vision of love, their hopes for romance, their desire for the intimacy of marriage. But since it was said of another human, this statement was a flat-out *lie*, a myth carefully and creatively packaged to ensnare and defeat.

If you believe that marriage, or the spouse you dream of, will complete you in this cinematic way, the reality of wedded life may seriously disappoint you. As remarkable as my husband is—and I have the honor of living with and loving a truly amazing man—he cannot make me whole.

Through the course of our marriage, Jeramy and I have been confronted by some deep wounds, some profound needs. But we have not been able to heal one another. God has certainly used Jeramy as an instrument of healing and love in my life, but the Lord has made it abundantly clear that *He* is ultimately the one working to restore and complete me.

Take a few moments to ponder these powerful and beautiful words from Ephesians 1:4-6:

Long before he laid down earth's foundations, he had us in mind, had settled on us as the focus of his love, to be made whole and holy by his love. Long, long ago he decided to adopt us into his family through Jesus Christ. (What pleasure he took in planning this!) He wanted us to enter into the celebration of his lavish gift-giving by the hand of his beloved Son.

Think about it . . . before the world sprang to life, God the Father had you in mind. He determined that you would be the "focus of his love, to be made *whole* and *holy*." He took great joy in arranging this and wanted you to know and come to it "by the hand of his beloved Son." Not by the hand of a great husband, not through the blessing of marriage, but through Jesus Christ, His Son. Again, Jesus may use marriage as part of the love that transforms us, making us whole and holy, but *He* is the source. He is the beginning and end.

I'd like to introduce you to a dear friend of mine, a woman who's mentored me and walked with me through some of the deepest valleys of my life. Kathy knows what it's like to expect a husband to satisfy, even to heal her. She assumed that marrying a godly man would make her whole. Instead, she discovered the Father's plan to make her complete through the love of His Son. As Kathy learned to look to Jesus, and not her husband, for wholeness and healing, she experienced deeper joy both in her relationship with God and in her marriage. Here's her story . . .

Hope for Our Gaping Holes
As told by Kathy Walton

The year I turned twenty-one was a big one for me. That year I made a decision that would seal my eternal destiny, the decision to follow Jesus. Just four months after that, I met my future husband, Dean, at a surprise party thrown for my twenty-first birthday. I was just drying off (having been tossed into a backyard pool, apparently to celebrate my adulthood) when a friend introduced me to two cadets from the Air Force Academy.

I struck up a conversation with the tall, dark, and handsome one. Even though I was "au naturel"—with no makeup, wet hair, and a borrowed set of dry clothes—Dean immediately put me at ease with his fun-loving, easygoing nature. Following the party, we went back to his apartment and talked until three in the morning. Before saying good night, Dean asked if I would like to go out with him the next weekend. I informed him I had already made plans to see a movie with my mom, but added that if he wanted to join us, he was more than welcome.

This marked the beginning of our friendship/dating relationship. Six months later, I flew out to California to meet Dean's parents and spend Christmas with them. During that week, we often went jogging together, enjoying the crisp northern California evenings. At the end of one of our runs, as we walked through a field, Dean stopped, looked at me, and said, "You'll never be ready to marry me, will you?"

Needless to say, this caught me completely off guard. Looking back, I realize that to Dean, I came across as incredibly independent and strong. But that was all I knew and the way I'd been raised. Dean had let his heart engage early in our relationship, and in some ways, he was waiting for me to catch up. His question revealed the frustration he felt with my self-sufficiency and semidetachment.

I flew home, confused about the future of our relationship. After returning to Colorado, very perplexed, I prayed fervently and searched the Scriptures, trying to discern God's will for Dean and me.

I thoroughly enjoyed our relationship, but on one level Dean was right: I hadn't seriously contemplated marriage. Over the next few days, as I continued to pray about it, I had a dream in which Dean and I were walking down a church aisle to be married. Jesus waited for us at the pulpit, ready to bless and oversee the ceremony. I couldn't quite explain it, but after that dream I felt peacefully confident that Dean was my future husband.

In February, we were engaged. Four months later, Dean and I married, and three years after the wedding, we brought our first child into the world.

Before Dean and I got married, I didn't think I had any expectations regarding marriage in general or what our relationship should look like. Nevertheless, I placed many unrealistic expectations on my husband. Though I seemed strong on the outside, I wanted Dean to make me feel whole and complete, to meet some deep emotional needs. Much later, I discovered only Christ could do this; but at the time, I looked to my husband.

Although I don't remember the specific conversation, we had a major fight within two weeks of our marriage. Looking back, I know our argument stemmed from misunderstanding mixed with the unattainable expectations I'd foisted on Dean. Our communication skills were pretty unrefined (to say it nicely!) in those days, and over the years that followed, communication continued to be the major area of struggle in our marriage. Though I loved Dean and believed he loved me, unresolved conflict or miscommunication between us could leave me feeling insecure and vulnerable.

Add to this the fact that I really didn't understand how to articulate my feelings or needs. It was all just so stuffed. With the intimacy of marriage, it was as if a deep, unquenchable yearning to feel loved and be complete burst open inside me. The problem was, I couldn't identify or express it.

So I communicated—a lot—about the things that "made sense" or "seemed right" to me: my desire to be obedient to the Lord and to follow Him, my hopes for a godly marriage. In retrospect I see that, at that time, my faith was a lot more about checking off boxes than real intimacy with Jesus; I lived under so many rules and masked expectations for myself. Naturally, this performance-oriented mentality infected my relationship with Dean.

Then came a real low point in my life, a time when I suffered from severe clinical depression. My husband hated to see me so downcast and thought his advice and help were sufficient to fix the problem. Though his intentions were good, I began to see that there was no way my husband could deliver me from my strongholds, some of which had held me captive since high school. The term "eating disorder" wasn't in common parlance back then, but I know now that I battled bulimia in my teenage years. The struggle continued through the first ten years of our marriage.

Before I got married, I just thought it was a self-control issue, or lack thereof. Until a few years into our marriage, I had never even heard of a clinical eating disorder. I really believed I could manage my problems and deal with them myself (part of my independent nature that also carried into my relationship with the Lord in those years). Because I lived out of a false "works-oriented" belief system, if I had a problem, I thought I could and had to take care of it. As you can imagine, this put incredible pressure on me. Not able to bear it all myself, I looked to Dean to help complete me and make me whole.

It was extraordinarily difficult for my husband to see me struggle and not be able to pull me out of the pit of depression and discouragement. Though I hadn't realized it walking down the aisle, I had entered marriage emotionally unhealthy.

Until I was delivered from the concerns that plagued me, I literally wasn't able to comprehend the love of my Savior. As one pastor described it, I had a hairball between my head and my heart. A gross analogy, perhaps, but quite apropos. You see, I knew many truths, could recite them, and talked about them with others. Somehow, though, my heart could not lay hold of them—especially the unconditional love of Jesus.

For those first years of my Christian life, I had desperately tried to earn His love and approval. And because I married only a short time after becoming a follower of Christ, I had this huge, gaping hole in my heart. Only Jesus could fill it, but for many years I expected Dean to. I wanted him to make me feel complete, significant, worthy, and attractive—there was a bottomless pit of need inside me.

True healing began when I faced my brokenness, when I recognized

I didn't have the answers or the strength to fight on my own. It took years of Christ-centered teaching, marriage retreats, and the insights of others to understand the roots of my insecurity and low self-esteem. Later, as I worked through some of the issues with a godly counselor, the Lord prompted me to ask forgiveness of my husband for placing so many unrealistic expectations on him in the early years of our marriage. I had wanted Dean to mend and heal me, but that was something only Jesus could do.

Once I truly experienced the love of God in a way I could apprehend, Dean was let off the hook . . . big time! God tangibly and powerfully revealed His love to me in a way I could understand it: He literally rescued me from the cords of death and set my feet upon a rock (as the psalms promise He will). Jesus filled me, satisfied me. And He continues to make me whole. Dean walks with me, sharpening and encouraging me, but I don't expect him to complete me anymore. I look to Christ for that and allow Dean to minister to me in the ways our Lord intended—as a leader, a partner, and my best earthly friend.

Worth the Trouble?

Though the details of their upbringings, past experiences, and present lives may differ from Kathy's, many singles believe they aren't whole until they find someone to marry, their "other half" as a spouse is sometimes called. Used in this context, what should be a beautiful image of marriage—"and the two shall become one" (Matthew 19:5, NASB)—actually becomes a punishing and horrid one.

I remember having lunch with a bright, beautiful, and talented young woman who told me that certain members of her family actually verbalized a belief that she wouldn't be a "complete Christian" until she married. This was especially hard for my friend to accept, as both her siblings had married and divorced. Were they somehow "more complete" than she, simply because they had walked down an aisle and said, "I do"?

Such thinking may sound ridiculous to you, but the lie that getting married makes someone whole, that it somehow completes him or her, is an incredibly powerful and prevalent one. This lie permeates many relationships (and eventually marriages), poisoning people's ability to be truly intimate with a toxic overdose of expectations and assumptions.

The deception is all around us. I recently received a junk e-mail from "Julia," who wrote the following:

I want to have my own family, a husband and kids. And to live in a cozy house, with a little yard where kids could play, and a little garden where we could plant roses. I dream to cook dinner for my family and enjoy watching how everyone likes the meals. I dream of taking our kids to school and picking them up after classes end. I dream that our family could go to the entertainment park and enjoy the rides and snacks. I dream of camping together and making barbecues on Saturdays. I dream of a loving, friendly, and sociable family, and I indeed hope that my future husband could be You, my dear. Please don't hesitate and make me wait any longer to become happy and to make you happy. Answer me at _____ [a website was provided here] and start building your happy future with me.

Nothing Julia wants — the house, the yard, the little garden, and a family to enjoy it with, even the entertainment park rides and snacks — is *wrong*. But the idea that these things will fulfill her (and the man who clicks on the underlined blue address) is patently false. Julia's words "don't hesitate and make me wait any longer to become happy and to make you happy" really break my heart, and it's not with sadness for her, necessarily. In fact, I doubt there's really even a "Julia" out there. These words were written by a marketing executive, someone who knows what lonely people ache for—companionship, comfort, *completion.*

But as I touched on in the opening paragraphs of this chapter, only God can meet these needs. Your relationship with the Lord will outlive every other connection you form on this earth. My own intimacy with God will outlast the marriage He's given me to enjoy here and now.

Whether or not we realize it, what we crave more than anything else is to be close to the God who made us. When that relationship is right, we tend not to make such severe demands on our friendships or our marriage. When we are intimate with the Almighty, we don't expect another person to compensate for the emptiness we sometimes feel.

Looking to another human to complete us will only lead to disappointment. It's simply inevitable, given that all of us are broken, that we wound and are wounded. But feeling disillusioned by a spouse's inability to meet all our needs can actually be a distinct blessing as well. Author Gary Thomas so aptly observed in *Sacred Marriage* that "approached in the right way, marriage can cause us to reevaluate our dependency on other humans for our spiritual nourishment, and direct us to nurture our relationship with God instead."[1]

With that in mind, I want to be certain that you understand: The Lord did not create us *only* for Himself. As Drs. Dan Allender and Tremper Longman III brilliantly expressed, "God does not exclusively fill the human heart. He made humankind to need more than himself. The staggering humility of God to make something that was not to be fully satisfied with the Creator and the creation is incomprehensible."[2] Not only does He want us to enjoy, delight in, and nurture other connections, but the Lord also designed us to *need* them. But for all of this to be right and in balance, He must remain at the center of our hearts.

No one else can complete us as He does. Why? Because in every single one of us, God designed the holiest and neediest place to be His alone. Only He can access this broken and incomplete part. No one can make us holy and whole as He has promised He will. In Christ alone can we experience fullness; only in Him can we know completeness.

And, if we're honest, this can be enormously frustrating. We were designed to need and long for relationships with other people. Yet our desire for intimacy *far outstrips* what we can receive from other humans, precisely because the same Designer who arranged this also determined that the most sensitive parts of us should be reserved for Him alone—"For in Christ the fullness of God lives in a human body, and you are complete through your union with Christ. He is the Lord over every ruler and authority in the universe" (Colossians 2:9-10, NLT). As with other areas of life—our health or our work, for instance—if we allow the frustration between what we need and what we can have to turn us back to God, who does complete and fulfill us, it will be worth the trouble.

The Time for Completion

Perhaps at this point in the book you're wondering if "happily ever after" even exists. Maybe it seems that marriage presents more challenges than comforts. If you feel this way, you're certainly in good company. In fact, the apostle Paul encouraged followers of Christ to honestly evaluate not only the way marriage enhances life but also how it complicates matters. Consider these challenging words from his first epistle to the Corinthians:

> *There's certainly no sin in getting married . . . All I am saying is that when you marry, you take on additional stress . . . and I want to spare you if possible.*

I do want to point out, friends, that time is of the essence. There is no time to waste, so don't complicate your lives unnecessarily. Keep it simple — in marriage, grief, joy, whatever. Even in ordinary things — your daily routines of shopping, and so on. Deal as sparingly as possible with the things the world thrusts on you. This world as you see it is on its way out.

I want you to live as free of complications as possible. When you're unmarried, you're free to concentrate on simply pleasing the Master. Marriage involves you in all the nuts and bolts of domestic life and in wanting to please your spouse, leading to so many more demands on your attention. The time and energy that married people spend on caring for and nurturing each other, the unmarried can spend in becoming whole and holy instruments of God. I'm trying to be helpful and make it as easy as possible for you, not make things harder. All I want is for you to be able to develop a way of life in which you can spend plenty of time together with the Master without a lot of distractions. (7:28-35)

There are no two ways about it: Marriage complicates life. It involves people in "all the nuts and bolts of domestic life" and in "wanting to please [their] spouse[s]," inevitably leading to "many more demands on [their] attention." And realistically, the more demands on your time and energy, the less of those resources you have available to devote to becoming "whole and holy instruments of God."

To be certain, there is *no sin* in getting married. Because Paul emphasized this, we must believe that it's possible to develop a way of life that is both attentive to the needs of marriage and also intimate with the Master. Through this passage, Paul simply revealed that, as a married person, it will be *more difficult* to balance these competing draws on your time and energy.

If you desire to be married, be prepared for complications,

distractions, and temptations. This is not to say that the single life is unfettered by such concerns—singles definitely face their own complex issues, diversions, and enticements. What singles usually do have, however, is more time to themselves. If they desire and maximize it, singles can spend more time alone, investing in a relationship with God: being completed, transformed, and made whole by Jesus.

Paul assumed that singles will use their time in this way: that they will eagerly and actively pursue healing, wholeness, and intimacy with Jesus (who makes these things possible). We know, however, that singles often do *not* choose to spend their time on such concerns. Like an unsuspected tide, the day-to-day stuff of living can overtake anyone—single or married. Or a person may be so consumed with the longing to get married that she loses track of the blessings of singleness.

When I married Jeramy, I was quite young. I had only recently begun to figure myself out and develop a genuinely intimate relationship with God. Before I got married, I savored long quiet times with Jesus and was thrilled by the ways He was making me whole and holy. (Hold on. Perhaps I should qualify that: I was *mostly* thrilled; sometimes, however, His loving refinement was quite painful.)

Early on in marriage, I discovered that such precious times alone with God would be *a lot* harder to come by. Jeramy would wake up—usually after me, since he's more of a night owl and I'm an early riser—stroll into the living room, where I was spending time with the Lord, and want to know (something as prosaic as!) what we were going to do for breakfast. It wasn't that he expected me to prepare his meal; he just wanted to share the morning hours with his wife. I tried to hide my frustration but wasn't very good at it. Actually, I could be downright mean if he interrupted my quiet time. So much for the wholeness and holiness God was forming in me! I felt like I was back at square one, selfish and easily angered, certainly not the peaceful contemplative I imagined myself to be.

Jeramy and I talked about what was going on. He wanted to give me time with the Lord, and I wanted to honor my husband—so we compromised. I started to get up earlier most days, but even on the days when he would come out while I was having a quiet time, Jeramy respected my desire to be with the Lord. For a while, this worked out just fine. But then we had children. I had no idea that I'd encounter the same complicated emotions and frustrations when my daughters would awaken during the middle of my time with God.

Looking back, I see how God used these circumstances to mold and shape me. He continued to form me in His likeness, to make me whole and complete, even when I was an exhausted mommy of two toddlers, only able to catch ten minutes of Bible reading or prayer.

Like Paul, my intention in discussing these issues is not to make things harder, nor is it my desire to scare you off from marriage. "All I want is for you to be able to develop a way of life in which you can spend plenty of time together with the Master without a lot of distractions" (1 Corinthians 7:35). If you choose to marry, simply remember that the road to wholeness may be a lot more complicated. There's no way for me to tell if it will be better or worse for you. I only suggest that it will likely be more complex for the simple reason that the vast majority of married people have less time alone than they did when they were single.

That's why it's my desire to encourage and challenge singles out there to invest *now*—before marriage—in really getting to know the Lord, in letting Him make you whole and complete. I'm certainly not the only writer who has issued this challenge; some have written entire books exploring why singles should, as well as how they can, make the most of their unmarried years.

Though the theme of seizing your singlehood is not the major subject of this book, I felt it important to share with you the simple fact that marriage complicates life. If you can squarely face this, simultaneously rejecting the idea that a relationship will automatically make you complete, whole, and satisfied, you'll be better equipped to embrace marriage.

If you're already married, you likely know what I mean about marriage complicating *everything*. For you, I issue this challenge: Invest the time that you do have alone in stillness with the Lord. If you need to, say no to some event. Don't answer the phone. Turn the television off. Do whatever it takes. Because Jesus longs for intimacy with you, if you purpose to surrender your time to Him, He *will* help you discover ways to find quiet and solitude.

Even if your time with Him is severely limited by work, a needy family, small children, or other demands, the time you do give Him will be multiplied exponentially. Our miracle-working God can, and will, do that because He desires to see you complete and satisfied. Marriage cannot do that for you, nor can your spouse. But He can. Will you let Him make you whole and holy as He desires to do?

A Genuine "Happily Ever After"

Despite the complications of marriage and the ever-present reality that a spouse cannot make us happy, whole, or complete, most people are still looking for their "happily ever after." In my mind, that isn't a bad thing. When I read one of the most popular premarital counseling books on the market, however, I was dismayed to find the following quotes highlighted with bold text:

> *We have been poisoned by fairy tales.*
> —*Anais Nin*[3]

> *"And they lived happily ever after" is one of the most tragic sentences in literature. It's tragic because it's a falsehood. It is a*

myth that has led generations to expect something from marriage that is not possible.

—Joshua Loth Liebman[4]

Let me say right off the bat that I know where the authors (not only those who quoted these words, but those who originated them) are coming from; I, too, am compelled to write because many people have developed unhealthy and unrealistic expectations for marriage. I absolutely agree that marriage *does not* equal "happily ever after," and hoping for a fairy-tale spouse who will bring happiness and fulfillment *is* a problem.

I also fear, however, that these words might be taken too extremely. Summarily dismissing fairy tales, along with the ideal of "happily ever after," is to attack the core of our humanity and the hope of the gospel as well. Fairy tales remind us that the world should have gone differently. They confirm our suspicions that love should win, virtue be rewarded, and purity prized. Of course, I'm not talking about the watered-down Disney tales that most of us have grown up with. I'm speaking of the genuine article.

For instance, did you know that in the original Cinderella story told by the Brothers Grimm, the young woman's *virtue* made her "happily ever after" possible? Or that Snow White's humility and purity made her stand out, especially in comparison to the haughty and envious queen? Beauty, whose love transformed the Beast into a man of noble character, was not simply a gorgeous and bookish brunette (as the animated version portrays her). Indeed, it was Beauty's character that enabled her first to bear with, and then ultimately love, Beast. Her name—Beauty—did not merely describe her physical attributes; it reflected deeper truths about the strength and splendor of her character.

We've been force-fed the lie that *physical beauty* and a *charming prince* make "happily ever after" possible for the fairy-tale princesses.

But stories like "Cinderella," "Snow White," and "Beauty and the Beast" were originally told not to inspire romantic idealism but rather to encourage young men and women to develop truth, goodness, and beauty in their character.

Though you may have grown up believing Disney had a corner on the fairy-tale market, many great writers have effectively used the "fairy story" genre to speak truth into our lives, capturing us with the chronicles of ordinary people experiencing extraordinary things.

One of the most popular Christian authors of all time, C. S. Lewis wrote fairy tales and also wrote about fairy tales. Lewis claimed these stories can awaken in us sensations we've never experienced. He said a good fairy tale

> may even be one of the greatest arts; for it produces works that give us (at the first meeting) as much delight (and on prolonged acquaintance) as much wisdom and strength as the works of the greatest poets. . . . It goes beyond the expression of things we have already felt. It arouses in us sensations we have never had before, never anticipated having, as though we had broken out of our normal mode of consciousness and "possessed joys not promised to our birth." It gets under our skin, hits us at a level deeper than our thoughts or even our passions, troubles oldest certainties till all questions are reopened, and in general shocks us more fully awake than we are for most of our lives.[5]

In other words, fairy tales help us grab hold of truths we might otherwise have missed.

In his book on Hollywood screenwriting, author and teacher Robert McKee concurred. McKee claimed people go to the movies (and I would add, people read fiction or spin tall tales) because they hope to find in someone else's story a truth that will enable them to understand their own. So often we long "to live [if only briefly] in a fictional reality that illuminates our daily reality."[6]

In many ways, we *need* fairy tales. Why? Because they help us develop vision — vision for the things that really count, vision for how life should be, and vision for the "happily ever after" that actually does await us.

As Christians, we believe in the ultimate happy ending — Christ will return, the Enemy will be punished, and Love will reign in eternity . . . for His are the kingdom and the power and the glory. This is no fairy tale. The glory of redemption, this promise of an imminent "happily ever after," is not simply wishful thinking for us. It is the defining reality of our lives.

If we do away completely with the vision of fairy tales, the dream of "happily ever after," as some people seem intent on recommending, we do ourselves more than a deep disservice. We take aim at the hope that genuinely sustains and *completes* us.

Sometimes, only the hope of heaven gets us through the refining processes of this life. Knowing that an ultimate "happily ever after" awaits us enables us to walk in this world with confidence and peace, particularly when circumstances might try to convince us otherwise.

I experienced a season like this after I delivered both of my daughters, when I suffered from unexpected postpartum depression. If I did not have a vision for the future, a vision for the happy ending I could look forward to, I may not have made it through those dark times. I know my "happily ever after" may not come on this earth. But the promises of God and the hope of an eternally abundant life with Him sustained me. One day, He will "wipe every tear from [our] eyes. Death . . . gone for good — tears gone, crying gone, pain gone — all the first order of things gone" (Revelation 21:4).

People fear they will be deceived or disappointed by believing that God *will* make things right. But this is what the Bible unashamedly calls us to claim. As Christian writer Simone Weil warned, "The danger is not lest the soul should doubt that there is any bread [God], but lest, by a lie, it should persuade itself it is not hungry. It can only persuade itself of this by lying, for the reality of its hunger is not a belief, it is a certainty."[7]

We hunger—insatiably—for a vision of the future. Without it, we cannot be made holy and whole as God intends. When we look to marriage to heal us, to complete us, it fails because finding "happily ever after" in another person is an illusion, a lie that persuades our soul that it is hungry for something other than what truly satisfies. "Happily ever after" as a concept, however, based on our hope in Jesus—the true Source—is life itself.

If we desire to be truly whole and complete, we must surrender our illusions. We must reject the notion that marriage, or a particular person, can fulfill us or heal our brokenness. Thank God we do not have to surrender the dream of "happily ever after." We were made for the greatest happy ending ever, and we cannot lose vision for it.

The Bible affirms our desperate need for vision. As Proverbs 29:18 proclaims, "Where there is no vision, the people *perish:* but he that keepeth the law, happy is he" (KJV, emphasis added). Lack of vision literally leads to death—the death of understanding, of trust, of hope. We cannot lose the vision for what God has promised, lest we miss what He has in store for us. *The Message* translation so beautifully renders this same verse:

> *If people can't see what God is doing,*
> *they stumble all over themselves;*
> *But when they attend to what he reveals,*
> *they are most blessed.*

I urge you: Catch and cling to a vision for the genuine "happily ever after" that awaits you. If you are not looking for marriage to be the ultimate end, you'll be better able to enjoy any happiness God might give you through a relationship. If you're not looking for marriage to complete you and make you whole, you'll be able to find healing and fulfillment in Christ, the only One who can make you who you long to be, who He created you to be. Don't lose sight of this vision, no matter what cynicism may tempt you to believe. May the truths of Scripture nourish and remind you, whether you walk through the valley or on the mountaintop.

Pressing On . . .

1. In her book *Keeping a Princess Heart in a Not-So-Fairy-Tale World*, author Nicole Johnson wrote, "Putting too much belief in one particular part of the truth distorts that truth."[8] How does this idea relate to what we've explored over the past several pages? What, if anything, is true about the idea, "When I get married, I'll be more complete"? What, if anything, do you recognize as a distortion of truth?

2. How does the idea that marriage complicates life strike you? Did the verses from 1 Corinthians 7, which explore this reality, affect you in any specific ways? In what practical ways can you begin to invest more time in your relationship with the Lord? What two things might you do to simplify your life over the next month, to disengage from those things that are unnecessarily taking time away from your walk with God?

3. In the course of our lives, we've all been wounded. One of my favorite songwriters compares this to a break in the "cup" that God designed to hold love inside us. Most of us know from experience that if we don't address the cracks we receive, they can create significant pain and distress in our relationships. For my friend Kathy, who shared her story in this chapter, an eating disorder and the method of "emotional stuffing" she learned before marriage were

cracks that seriously affected her relationship with Dean. Kathy found healing in Christ, who is the Source of all healing. What cracks or breaks might mar your cup of love? Have you invited Jesus into these broken places, to heal and restore them? If so, how has He faithfully done so? If not, how might you move forward in healing?

4. After we've been hurt, we often experience seasons of despair, insecurity, or concern for the future. Situations like these can make us feel incomplete, broken, and hopeless. God promises mercy and grace to us during such times: "He will not break the bruised reed, nor quench the dimly burning flame. He will encourage the fainthearted, those tempted to despair. He will see full justice given to all who have been wronged" (Isaiah 42:3, TLB). Are there any circumstances in your life that this verse speaks to? If so, how could genuinely living in this hope transform both your situation and the emotions connected to it? How do you think these circumstances might fit into God's healing process, His plan to make you whole and complete? Read Philippians 1:6 for encouragement.

5. As we discussed, catching and clinging to a vision for the hope of our "happily ever after" is essential. Looking forward to the day when all tears will be wiped away and when death will reign no more helps us to endure some of the difficult seasons of life. God has given us other promises regarding our sorrows as well, and one of my favorites comes from Psalm 56:8 — "You keep track of all my sorrows. You have collected all my tears in your bottle. You have recorded each one in your book" (NLT). How does it make you feel that God keeps track of your sorrows, that He collects your tears and records each one? How can this relate to your expectations for and disappointment in romance and marriage?

THREE

I Won't Feel Lonely Anymore

LONELY WINDS BLOW THROUGH each and every life. Indeed, loneliness seems to be a universal human experience and, among singles, one of the chief complaints. Unfortunately, a big reason many people hope to marry in the future is to assuage the ache of a lonely heart.

Now please don't misread me: I say "unfortunately" not because it's a mistake for people to want to deal with their loneliness; I completely understand why people hope to sort out their feelings of isolation. I applaud those who want to get to the root of their emotions and manage them. It's simply problematic how many singles assume that getting married will instantaneously take away their feelings of loneliness and alienation.

For others, like my dear friend Cameron, loneliness before marriage might not have been as big a concern. Sure, she had lonely times, insecure times. Doesn't every adolescent? Cameron never imagined, however, that her husband's swing-shift schedule would bring up some deep-rooted issues in her heart, leaving her a lonesome newlywed. But I'll let Cameron fill you in on the rest of her story . . .

Not Just Filling the Void
As told by Cameron Germann

Brian and I dated in fits and starts. We first met after an Army-Navy football game, at a banquet for Christians. I was sixteen and in high school, helping at the banquet because my family served in a ministry at the military academy. Brian was twenty-one, a midshipman at Annapolis. He says it was love at first sight; I thought all his attention toward me, a perfect stranger, was kind of weird. That didn't stop me from going out with him, though.

In fact, Brian and I dated for a year after that. Eventually, we went our separate ways, supposedly "to grow up a bit." We didn't get back together until I was twenty-one and he was twenty-six. At the time, I was living as a short-term missionary in Papua New Guinea, and he was stationed in Japan (but that's another story). Because we were separated by such distance, we mostly "dated" and got to know each other via letters. When we were finally engaged—and both living in Colorado—we'd been in the same city for only a month and a half of our two-year courtship! We got married on a gorgeous summer day, and our life together began. After our honeymoon, Brian went back to his Navy job, and I worked part time while finishing my college degree.

We loved the Lord and one another; it seemed we were off to a great start. Still, there was one pretty obvious problem. Maybe I felt like we needed to make up for lost time; perhaps it was just the differences in our personalities (I'm an extrovert; he's pretty introverted) . . . I don't know. It just seemed like I wanted to spend every waking minute together, while Brian was much more okay with his swing-shift, work-straight-through-Thursday-night-and-into-Sunday-morning schedule.

My husband, apparently, was fine. I battled loneliness. Sometimes I experienced an inexplicable but overwhelming sense that I didn't measure up. I know it seems a bit extreme, but that's how I felt. Insecurity issues from my high school and college days resurfaced—fear of not having someone to hang with on the weekends and the assumption that when I got married all those feelings would go away. I really believed that when I married, I'd always have someone to be with; I'd never be the odd man out again; I'd never feel painfully alone.

I had made the transition from family life (precollege) to dorm life, from intern life (right after college) back to family life (for a few months before I got married). Never had I lived all on my own, away from intense community. I missed companionship, especially on the weekends when people (the cosmic "they") say you should be with someone, relaxing and having fun. I felt a great loss and had to do a major reality check of my expectations, assumptions that probably shouldn't have been there in the first place.

Before I married Brian, I imagined that marriage would equal being with my best friend . . . all the time. I thought we would hang out and talk forever and ever; we'd go on long walks, understand each other, and be there for each other. I knew marriage would be hard—my parents had drilled that into my head!—but I don't recall hearing that it would often be lonely. That hurt. For a while, it felt like I had a cotton ball in my heart, sapping life and joy from deep inside me.

Brian and I talked about my expectations, but at first, our discussions didn't go so well. He probably felt like I was too demanding and wanted him to meet my every need for togetherness or connection. Brian craved space on the weekends he did have off; I wanted every minute to be "the two of us." Trouble was, I felt even lonelier when he got frustrated with my extroverted needs.

Over the course of our first two years of marriage, our fights always seemed to circulate back to this struggle and finding a way to solve it. Since I knew this was a huge point of contention for us, I could have tried to find other outlets for fellowship, thereby giving Brian the alone time he longed for. Instead, the tension of his needing space and my feeling lonely continued to create major friction in our relationship.

The reality was, my husband couldn't be "my everything." I never thought I would put him in that position (I was a strong and competent woman, after all!), but I definitely needed to learn not to expect Brian to meet all of my heart needs. Instead, I discovered I could turn to God, as well as other practical solutions He might lead me to. These included hanging out with single girlfriends or other military wives, who frequently felt lonely like I did. Often, I got to be a blessing to someone else who needed encouragement or a friend to hang with after a tough day; those times were (and still are) a gift from the Lord.

While we were processing all of this, Brian and I both had to make some compromises. He tried to honor me and let me know when he'd be working through the weekend or when he had other plans. That way, I could make arrangements for myself way in advance. Scheduling ahead of time helped me prepare for the possibility of isolating and lonely feelings.

Another practical help God gave Brian and me came through personality profiling. As we learned—through a test called the Myers-Briggs Type Indicator (MBTI)—the ways in which God had wired us to be unique and to approach the world and relationships differently, we saw that we really needed distinct things. I now know that my husband must get time alone; otherwise, he's not a happy camper. Brian knows that I must get time with people (especially him); without that, I'm not at my best. Understanding this makes it easier for me to serve Brian, giving him the space that allows him to be the man God created him to be. The reverse *is true for the "people time" I crave and require.*

I never imagined that I would feel so lonely and isolated in my marriage. And because I'm such a people person, there were many painful times during our first two years. But today, I see how God powerfully used the disappointments and disillusionment of those early months to teach me more about Himself, showing me that all my needs can be met in Him. He is my security and my all in all. I can't look to anyone else to satisfy me, not even the great and godly husband He's given me. When I do get sad and lonely, I now know to run to Jesus, laying those feelings at His feet. And that experiential knowledge is such a gift!

God's also shown me over and over that the success of my marriage often depends on my own growth. I joked right after the wedding that being married is like having a permanent accountability partner (one you can't gloss anything over with). The lonely times of our first two years showed me that I needed not only to find my total satisfaction in the Lord and His love for me but also to be honest with God, Brian, and myself about my needs for companionship. This allowed me to be proactive in responding to my heart needs, not merely to fill the void of loneliness but to authentically acknowledge them and hopefully, through my weakness, bless others in similar situations. In turn, Jesus has richly blessed me.

What Are You Cultivating?

Cameron's story brings out some very important points about loneliness, as well as the standard human responses to it. Like most of us, Cameron looked first to another person — to another *human* — to meet her need for companionship. This may appear a stupidly simple detail to note, but think about it: Isn't this actually a rather significant fact for those of us who claim fellowship with Christ?

We, who declare our undying love for Jesus, *say* that He is our all in all, but when push comes to shove, when we feel isolated and alone, how many of us text our best friend, call up our boyfriend, or track down our spouse in whatever way we can? Perhaps we don't run as hard after the Savior as one might think we do after listening to us sing on Sunday morning.

Another interesting aspect of my friend's experience is what loneliness meant to her. Cameron's feelings communicated something to her about what she was worth. Did you notice that? If she didn't have someone to be with on the weekend, she wasn't "cool" or "okay." Of course, these were just her feelings, not the reality. I would personally love to spend *any* weekend with Cameron, and all of her friends would say the same. But, like Cam, we've all experienced the power of feelings and how wickedly they can twist the truths that we are beloved, cherished, accepted, and valued beyond measure.

Loneliness often speaks distorted and venomous lies into the lives of men and women, married or single: You're not worth being with . . . no one wants to be with you . . . and no one ever will . . . you'll be alone *forever.* These toxic beliefs can slowly infect every aspect of a person's life, eroding confidence, destroying peace, stealing joy.

Again, the natural reaction of most people is to look to another person to erase their lonely feelings, to bridge the gap between alienation and connection. But the lies loneliness speaks can never be confronted simply by getting married. You won't suddenly feel worthy or loved because you have a ring on your fourth finger. Ask Cameron. Ask any husband or wife. In a tragically ironic way, being lonely as a married person is often more painful than being lonely when single—you're not "supposed" to be lonely when you have "someone."

On a positive note, as Brian and Cameron worked through their expectations and desires, they learned three distinct lessons about dealing with loneliness, each of which may apply to your own life.

The first involves striving to understand yourself and the people with whom you're in close relationship. We'll take a closer look at this later, but it's essential to note that as Brian and Cameron discovered how their personalities influenced the ways they related and the needs they had, the times Cameron felt lonely diminished considerably.

The second lesson concerns planning ahead. Brian and Cameron found that if they scheduled in advance, preparing for times when he would be away or when he might need or want some space, they avoided a lot of unnecessary heartache. For singles or spouses who know that certain times or seasons spark loneliness for them, planning in advance is a good idea as well. Lining up family, friends, and, most importantly, spiritual retreats with the Lord will give you something to look forward to, as well as something to forestall potentially isolating emotions.

Here is the third, closely related lesson Cameron gleaned from experiencing loneliness in the early days of her marriage: Loneliness can be cultivated into something beautiful by and for God if you give Him the chance and decide to labor with Him. I urge you, my friend: Decide—here and now—to peer into the pain loneliness may bring you, to find out what it's there for, to discover why God's allowed it and what He might be saying to you through it. As you courageously lean into the lonely winds and stretch out your arms, you will find Him there.

That's What the Lonely Is For

> Picture your hope, your heart's desire —
> As a castle that you must keep
> In all of its splendor, it's drafty with lonely
> This heart is too hard to heat
>
> When I get lonely ah, that's only a sign
> Some room is empty, and that room is there by design
> If I feel hollow — that's just my proof that there's more
> For me to follow — that's what the lonely is for

Is it a curse or a blessing this palace of promise
When the empty chill makes you weep
With only the thin fire of romance to warm you
These halls are too tall and deep

When I get lonely ah, that's only a sign
Some room is empty, and that room is there by design
If I feel hollow — that's just my proof that there's more
For me to follow — that's what the lonely is for

But, you can seal up the pain, build walls in the hallways
Close off a small room to live in
But those walls will remain, and keep you there always
And you'll never know why you were given . . . why you
*   were given the lonely . . .*

From the deep of your dreams, the height of your wishes
The length of your vision to see, the hope of your heart
Is much bigger than this
For it's made out of what might be

When I get lonely ah, that's only a sign
Some room is empty, and that room is there by design
If I feel hollow — that's just my proof that there's more
For me to follow — that's what the lonely is for[1]

Before I came across this wonderful song, I hadn't wondered if loneliness was a curse or a blessing. If you'd have asked me prior to listening to Wilcox's ballad, I'd have told you that I flat-out *hated* feeling lonely and scrupulously avoided it at all costs. A blessing . . . loneliness? No way!

Yet David Wilcox clearly believes loneliness is there for a reason. He called it a "palace of promise," a room that's "there by design." When we feel hollow, he revealed, it proves there's something *more* for us to follow.

But here's the problem: Do we usually respond to the call of loneliness in this way? No. Instead, as the empty chills of life make us weep, we try to warm ourselves with the "thin fire of romance." It doesn't take a singer-songwriter like Wilcox to tell us "these halls are too tall and deep"; we instinctively *know* that romantic relationships can't meet all our needs.

Truly, we were designed with lonely rooms, palaces of promise that only He who is "much bigger than this" can fill and warm and heal. So often we are an aching, empty, lonely people, yearning to be filled. But is this necessarily so? Is there no other way to face and follow the hollow hauntings of loneliness?

I appreciate how author and speaker Tim Hansel echoes the truths of Scripture and the poignant wisdom of artists like David Wilcox. In his piercing and beautiful book *Through the Wilderness of Loneliness*, Hansel observed,

> *Loneliness is a gift from God. A gift that opens up our heart to yearn for His peace. It is a longing for a deeper experience of His presence. . . . Loneliness can also be an unexpected invitation to discover God's love and mercy at a previously unexplored level. . . . Believe it or not, loneliness is one of the most powerful ways for us to fully understand and experience that . . . God made us for Himself. We were designed for a relationship with the Father. . . . Sometimes the problem is that we are too full of ourselves — perhaps because we don't truly believe that God is enough, that His reality is sufficient on a daily, practical level. So we pursue our distractions and are on the way to becoming "functional atheists," no longer believing that God can fill our empty hearts.[2]*

"Some room is empty, and that room is there by design." God made us for Himself, for relationship with Himself. But sometimes we're "too full of ourselves," too distracted by the thin fire of romance that we're using to try to warm our lonely hearts, that we end up living like atheists. We may not mean to, but—whether or not we claim to believe in God—if we *act* as if our happiness and fulfillment is up to us, we are functioning as atheists do.

Instead, if loneliness invites us to open our hearts to a deeper peace and more intimate experience of God's living presence, if it woos us onward and upward, causing us to explore God's mercy and love in a way we've never done before, we can sense that it is indeed a gift and a grace to be alone.

Certainly, loneliness can make us *feel* abandoned and isolated, but usually this isn't reality. Again, our feelings can deceive. Most often, equipped with His perspective, we can see lonely times as opportunities to encounter—on a new and deeper level—the only One who can heal the empty and anguished places in our hearts.

Of course, there are times when we are genuinely rejected and forsaken. God can help us walk through these valleys of shame and grief. He can also enable us to distinguish when the loneliness we feel is an emptiness that He's asking us to *feel* rather than fill. Sometimes it's important that we remain "empty" in our loneliness. Do we ever delay the gracious healing God has for us, trying to sate our own aching hearts?

Lonely times can seem like the long months of winter—bare, harsh, and bleak. Yet, as Hansel pointed out, deep growth often occurs during seasons of apparent barrenness. He painted a striking word picture while detailing a winter scene that arrested his imagination one morning, reminding him what's often happening through the "dead" months of a lonely winter:

I walked along a pathway which cut a swath through high grass and hay bales. On the ridge were silhouetted trees, leafless, waiting for spring. Somehow when we see trees like this, we think they are dead; the truth is that they have just pulled their life inward, condensed it in an appropriate economy. All of its energies are pulled into a solitary life within to a deeper core. It is a restrained strength. Less expressive, but no less beautiful.[3]

During seasons of loneliness and isolation—whether perceived or actual[4]—God sometimes calls us to pull our life inward, condensing our energies in appropriate economy and restrained strength (this, interestingly, is one of the definitions of *meekness,* and part of the fruit of the Spirit, as defined by Galatians 5:22-23). It may be less expressive, Hansel wrote, than the buds of spring—in this case, the joys of outward friendship and fellowship—but it is no less beautiful.

As long as we are in this human frame, we will deal with loneliness. God will not magically zap the holes in our hearts, patching them neatly. He will, however, give our winters meaning, our solitary times purpose, our lonely scars reason.

Let me ask you this: Why do you think God left an imprint of the nails on Jesus' hands and feet when He raised Him from the dead? Why didn't the Father patch His Son perfectly? Why did He leave the scars? While there are many wonderful (and theologically rich) reasons we could explore, here's one to consider: "The peace that we look for is [always] a *presence* rather than a principle."[5]

Jesus' physical scars remind us that we can never be without Him. The idea of Him is not enough; knowing about Him is not enough. We need His body, broken, His blood shed for us. The Phillips translation renders Philippians 4:5, "Never forget the nearness of your Lord." Isn't that a great reminder, especially when we feel isolated, when those we love are anywhere but "near"?

He is near, even when the cold winds of loneliness blow through us. And isolation can lead us into His arms. In this way, loneliness truly can be a gift. The question is, will we allow it to be? For if we want to experience the rich blessings of solitude, we must cultivate our emptiness, transforming it into something beautiful, as Cameron has learned to do and as many before and with her have too.

Somewhat paradoxically, for those who love and follow Jesus, the "answer" to loneliness is aloneness. This strikes us as paradoxical, perhaps, because to ease the pain of loneliness, connection *is* imperative. Most people assume, however, that this connection has to be with another human; it does not.

Indeed, as the incredibly wise writer Henri Nouwen once noted, to live a genuinely spiritual life, we must first find the courage to press into the desert of loneliness and convert it, by "gentle and persistent efforts," into a "garden of solitude."[6]

The Garden of Solitude

Turning loneliness into a garden of solitude . . . what in the world does that mean? Is that even something I want? Gentle and persistent efforts? I don't know about you, but gentleness and persistence really aren't my strong points. And what about courage? Bravery is in short supply when I'm feeling alone and isolated. If this is the core of the spiritual life, as Nouwen suggested, I may be in for some serious trouble. Do you feel the same?

Perhaps it would help us first to identify the difference between loneliness and solitude. Since one of the goals of this book is to align our thoughts with the Lord's, to think straight under the guidance and direction of the Holy Spirit, it would be best to find out what loneliness and solitude actually look like.

Loneliness is feeling alone, whether or not one actually happens to be alone (case in point, you can feel terribly lonesome at a party with a hundred or more people). Solitude is actually being alone, but still feeling full. Solitude is quiet and focused; loneliness feels frenetic and frantic. Loneliness concentrates on externals, solitude on the "inner adventure." Loneliness listens to what others think and say about you. Solitude inclines to what God has said from the beginning. Loneliness focuses on want, on deficiency, on lack. Solitude rejoices in presence, provision, and purpose.[7]

To evaluate how these things play out in our lives, we need the Lord's grace as well as His daily guiding presence. Learning the difference between loneliness and solitude also requires time and a willingness to practice—commodities we often find in short supply.

Consequently, choice plays an incredibly important role in the movement from loneliness to solitude. Whether single or married, you'll likely need to decide—not just once, but again and again—to surrender lonely times to the Lord. In doing so, you will discover the invaluable benefits of being trained by God to live in the contented ease of solitude rather than the restless ache of loneliness. These benefits include balance, freedom, and peace.

Peace becomes ours as we pursue a new level of intimacy with Christ. By clinging to Him in our aloneness, we grow closer to Him. In God's presence, our perspectives are reordered, and we can view the circumstances of life with greater insight. Freedom follows, a freedom to engage with the needs and desires of others. When lonely, we rarely look beyond those things or experiences that will satisfy our own immediate needs. Solitude teaches us the significance—and transforming power—of listening to the lives of those around us. Whatever stage of life you are in, these are priceless lessons.

Along with the peace and freedom of solitude, we also discover balance. God designed each of us to crave and genuinely need Him. But, as we noted in chapter 2, the Lord also created us with a deep and persistent desire for relationship with other humans. We, quite literally, *need* other people.

Establishing a garden of solitude with the Lord includes developing a perspective that balances our needs for intimacy with Him and connectedness with others. He is our first love. Before any other, we turn to Him. We do not, however, have to feel guilty when we need others, as if we are somehow betraying the Lord or questioning His sufficiency. Instead, we can begin to evaluate our motives. The ache of loneliness compels people to seek their own relief; the balance of solitude enables them to pursue closeness with the Lord and fulfilling connections with other people—at the right time, for appropriate reasons, and in fitting ways.

Wouldn't it be great if, before you got married, you learned to listen to the words and worlds of others, to live from the tranquil center of your heart rather than being driven by loneliness? Wouldn't it be wonderful, whether you're married or single, to stop being motivated primarily by the cravings of your own needs and to start being free, balanced, and at peace?

Most of us, however, do not respond to loneliness in these creative and life-giving ways. Instead, in an attempt to quiet the sting of isolation, we turn to diversions and amusements. We choose distraction, thereby distancing ourselves from the quiet center of our hearts, where the Lord would teach and nourish us. The consequences are deep and pervasive.

In his book *Reaching Out,* Henri Nouwen so wisely observed,

As long as we are trying to run away from our loneliness we are constantly looking for distractions with the inexhaustible need to be . . . kept busy. . . . Then our life becomes a spastic and often destructive sequence of actions and reactions pulling us away from our inner selves. . . . The movement from loneliness to solitude should lead to a gradual conversion from an anxious reaction to a loving

*response. Loneliness leads to quick . . . reactions which make us pris-
oners of our constantly changing world. But in solitude of heart we
can listen to the events of the hour . . . and slowly "formulate," give
form to, a response that is really our own. In solitude we can pay
careful attention to the world and search for an honest response.*[8]

This, perhaps, is why the psalmist enjoined us to be still and *know*
(experience on a heart, soul, and mind level) that He is God (see Psalm
46:10). In solitude we discover that we are truly never alone. These are
not just words that people toss around in Sunday school to make kids
feel better. These are the truths we need to stake our lives on.

As you seek this truth, beware that feelings may mislead you.
Loneliness doesn't usually travel by itself. It often partners with parasite emotions such as guilt, shame, and discouragement; attaches itself
to anxiety and fear; and makes you feel that everything is wrong when
things might be all right. That's why it's extremely important for you to
recognize exactly what you're feeling.

You may have been told in the past not to think with your feelings,
and that really is excellent advice; when we make decisions based only
on our emotions, things can get terribly confused. But when we don't
feel our feelings, things can also get horribly confused. God made us
emotional creatures, and we must be able to feel our feelings, even the
negative ones such as loneliness and anxiety.

The process of acknowledging, feeling, and appropriately express-
ing our emotions—the most distressing ones included—is part of
what God uses to move us through and beyond feelings of isolation.
We often find the fullness of solitude in feeling and working through
(the word *express* literally means to "push out") emotions that we might
be tempted to ignore. Through this process, we may also see how God
uses solitude as a gift. It's far easier to wade through our feelings in
seasons of quiet aloneness than in times of busy noisiness.

The Lord may inspire you to express yourself through journaling, artistic creativity, time in nature, or some other means. No matter what He uses, you can be sure that the *journey* is as important—and as valuable—as the result . . . a peaceful contentment in solitary times.

I'm not going to pretend this is easy, though. It requires *determined courage* to enter the desert of loneliness and trust that God is there, that He will work with you gently and persistently, transforming your isolation into a garden—a beautiful place—of solitude instead. But this work of cultivation and nurturing will be one of the richest investments of time and energy you can make.

I pray that you can do it when you are single, before you meet the person with whom you'd like to spend the rest of your life. But if you're already dating or married, there's still time to learn these lessons. Press in, no matter where you are, and let the cultivation begin.

What Kind of Companionship Do You Crave?

As I mentioned earlier, it was extraordinarily important for my friend Cameron to determine how her unique personality fed into her struggle with loneliness, as well as how her husband's temperament interfaced with her own. Brian and Cameron used a particular personality profiling tool to help them, but there are many that might prove useful for you. I've listed a couple that I'm particularly fond of in the Notes section of this book.[9]

Whether or not you ever take a personality test, it would be a wonderful thing for you to know what kind of companionship best meets your needs. In order to discover this, begin with some simple questions, such as "Do you consider yourself more of an extrovert or an introvert?"

But maybe I'm getting ahead of myself. Perhaps you're unfamiliar with the actual definitions of these terms. If you'd like to sort out how to deal with loneliness, it would be a good idea to know not only what words like this mean but also how they specifically relate to your personality and wiring.

According to a superbly straightforward article by professor Carol Bainbridge,

> Most people believe that an extrovert is a person who is friendly and outgoing. While that may be true, that is not the true meaning of extroversion. Basically, an extrovert is a person who is energized by being around other people. This is the opposite of an introvert who is energized by being alone. Extroverts tend to "fade" when alone and can easily become bored [or restless or lonely] without other people around. When given the chance, an extrovert will talk with someone else rather than sit alone and think. In fact, extroverts tend to think as they speak, unlike introverts who are far more likely to think before they speak. Extroverts often think better when they are talking. Concepts just don't seem real to them unless they can talk about them; reflecting on them isn't enough.[10]

Looking at these definitions, it's probably easy to see why Brian and Cameron experienced tension in their relationship. Cameron, a self-proclaimed extrovert, "fades" when alone. She feels energized and alive around people, especially Brian, whom she loves best. Brian, a classic introvert, needs alone time to recharge and renew. He can't continuously be around others; that's when Brian starts to wither. Where do you fall on a spectrum like this?

Dr. Emerson Eggerichs, a Christian psychologist and best-selling author, described another way people differ in their need for companionship. In his excellent book *Love and Respect*, Eggerichs made an important distinction between face-to-face companionship and side-by-side companionship:

I learned about this . . . need for face-to-face connection from my daughter, Joy, when she was just four years old. One evening I put her to bed, and I lay there with her for a few moments to help her get to sleep. The room was pitch black, and Joy was talking as usual—little Miss Motor-Mouth. Neither of us could see the other in the darkness. As she was talking, suddenly she said, "Daddy, look at me!" Then her little hands reached over and grabbed my face, forcing me to look toward her. Already at this age, even in the dark, she sensed that Daddy wasn't looking, and if he wasn't looking, then he wasn't listening![11]

Eggerichs identified this as a particularly feminine quality, noting that at any given coffee shop, you can find women engaged in conversation *face-to-face*, eagerly leaning across the small round tables to talk as closely as possible. Men, he claimed, opt more often for side-by-side companionship. They'll place their chairs facing out, still speaking to one another, mind you, but not usually face-to-face.

I don't necessarily think that these have to be predominantly male or female traits.[12] You may be a woman who values side-by-side companionship much more than face-to-face companionship. This may be a function of your time of life, your personality, some combination of the two, or a factor I cannot predict. Or you may fit into the more stereotypical portrait of a woman. That's okay too. What's important is that you get to know yourself, how you're wired, and how loneliness affects *you*.

The more self-aware you are, the better able you'll be to face the lonely winds that blow through your life. You'll also be equipped to more lovingly relate to others, whether or not you marry. If you think about it, there's really nothing to lose since knowing the way God has specifically created you both honors Him and prepares you for the future. I challenge and encourage you to invest in and commit to this.

Pressing On . . .

1. Loneliness sometimes sneaks up on us. It does this by striking not when we're empty (and we might expect it) but when we're too full. Think back on a time in your life when an overly busy schedule or an excessively demanding season left you feeling isolated and lonesome. During this time, how might cultivating a garden of solitude with the Lord have helped you?

2. When I was engaged, I recall being so excited to think that I wouldn't have to say good-bye to Jeramy anymore. We could spend all day and night together, I thought. Ten years later, I realize how severely I underestimated the difficulties of coordinating two schedules, especially when kids are part of the equation (I guess that makes more than two schedules, doesn't it?). Singles sometimes believe, as I did, that once they get married, they'll have all the time in the world with their beloved. How might this play into the experience many young married people have with loneliness?

3. The book of Psalms resounds with cries of loneliness. The next time you feel isolated and alienated, turn to the words of the ancient Hebrew poets. Psalm 25 can be a particularly beautiful prayer to use:

   > Turn to me and be gracious to me,
   > For I am lonely and afflicted.
   > The troubles of my heart are enlarged;
   > Bring me out of my distresses.
   > Look upon my affliction and my trouble . . .
   > Do not let me be ashamed, for I take refuge in You.
   > (verses 16–18,20, NASB)

Spend a few moments looking in a concordance or using a Bible dictionary to find at least one other reference to loneliness in the book of Psalms. Now find a promise of God's presence and provision. If you struggle with loneliness often, consider writing these verses on notecards and carrying them with you, placing them on the mirror in your bathroom, or memorizing them for maximum effect.

4. As this chapter discussed, if we hope to understand our situation and move beyond it, we've got to work through our emotions. Think back to the last time you felt extremely lonely. What parasite emotions (guilt, shame, fear) piggybacked on the lonesome feelings you had? How might you identify and separate those feelings next time so that you can deal with them individually?

5. Sometimes it's good to be reminded what kind of God we serve. Yahweh is a father to orphans, a defender of the weak and helpless; He sets the lonely in families. Meditate on the words of Psalm 68, which proclaim,

> Let the righteous be glad; let them exult before God;
> Yes, let them rejoice with gladness.
> Sing to God, sing praises to His name;
> Lift up a song for Him who rides through the deserts,
> Whose name is the LORD, and exult before Him.
> A father of the fatherless and a judge for the widows,
> Is God in His holy habitation.
> God makes a home for the lonely. (verses 3-6, NASB)

What do these words mean to you?

FOUR

Life Will Be
So Much Better

JUST NINE MONTHS INTO Blake and Megan's marriage, the unthinkable happened. In an instant, and over the course of two trying years, one word turned this couple's life upside down and inside out: *cancer.*

At twenty-four years of age, Blake—young, vibrant Blake—discovered that the pain in his ankle (the nagging ache he and Megan originally attributed to an old sports injury) was actually osteosarcoma, a rare form of aggressive bone cancer. Megan and her husband spent the next two years in and out of hospitals and doctors' offices, waging war on Blake's illness through chemotherapy and surgeries.

This wasn't what either of them expected for their newlywed years; this wasn't what they bargained for. At times, the cancer threatened to take not only Blake's life but the health and strength of their marriage, too. Thankfully, it didn't. Instead, these incredibly difficult circumstances have drawn Megan and Blake into deeper intimacy with one another and with God. What could have consumed them, God has used to refine and expand Blake and Megan.

Because she has squarely faced some of the most challenging misconceptions about marriage, I asked Megan to share her story with you. Like many young brides, Megan believed that when she married, life would only get better. She'd have someone to share the rest of her life with, someone who would always be there for her. As Megan describes what it's like to see these assumptions crumble, then to watch God's mercy poured out in abundance, I pray her words will encourage you.

Not Quickly Broken
As told by Megan Vandergeest

Needless to say, Blake's diagnosis completely shocked us. One day my husband was a healthy, strong, athletic guy with what we thought was tendinitis, and the next day he was a cancer patient with a tumor in his ankle. Everything changed after that fateful doctor's visit.

At the time, Blake and I were still enjoying our status as newlyweds, feeling like the entire world was at our doorstep and reveling in the wonderful, fun, exciting adventure of life together. We had been talking about moving, buying a house, finding new jobs, going back to school. So many possibilities seemed open to us . . . we really felt invincible!

With the oncologist's words, all our big plans came to a screeching halt. Of course, the strongest underlying fear was for Blake's life, but as a couple, we were also afraid of the many ways his illness would affect our day-to-day life: our finances, our intimacy, our future.

Because his cancer was already stage III, Blake's doctors prescribed a very aggressive, very long regimen of chemotherapy. My husband underwent six cycles of chemo over about three months in an attempt to shrink the tumor; unfortunately, this plan didn't work as well as the oncologists had hoped.

They then prescribed (and Blake endured) a bone transplant and skin-graft surgery to remove the tumor, which meant a month of bedrest and recovery, followed by a few more months in a wheelchair and on crutches. Once his body had recovered enough to tolerate more, Blake went through another ten cycles of intense chemotherapy, designed to obliterate any remaining cancer and reduce its chances of coming back.

During each chemo treatment, Blake spent anywhere from three to six days in the hospital. At home, he felt incredibly sick and exhausted, sometimes sleeping for twenty hours a day. On the days he had strength and energy, Blake tried to work. Ultimately, however, the cancer forced him to take an extended medical leave.

As you can imagine, this was an incredibly trying time for us.

Blake lost his hair, his appetite, and his physical strength. With the chemo, he battled constant exhaustion. Surgery left him virtually immobile. Meanwhile, I had to balance my relatively new full-time job and the even newer role of full-time caretaker, which included keeping track of filling and refilling prescriptions, shuttling Blake to doctor's appointments and treatments, learning how to administer injections and various medications, figuring out what he could tolerate to eat or drink, and then taking care of cooking, maintaining our home and finances, and more.

Emotionally, Blake and I gravitated toward extremes. Blake felt weak, vulnerable, helpless, and (I suspect) pretty emasculated. Frustrated that he constantly had to sit back and let people do things for him, things he used to do quite easily on his own, Blake became unlike himself—quiet and weepy at times, a bit needy and clingy at others. I went the opposite direction: Trying to put feelings aside, I became distant, self-reliant, focused on getting things done. Though I hated acknowledging it, I also felt quietly resentful that I had to take care of so much. I knew the cancer wasn't Blake's fault, and I certainly didn't want to blame him. My heart ached with love and grief for Blake, but I also desperately missed the role he used to fill. I never realized I had such a strong vision of what marriage should look like.

Before meeting Blake, I hadn't given much conscious thought to what I expected from marriage. God did bless me with a great model for marriage in my own parents, though. Through them I saw marriage as a team effort: shared responsibilities, a lot of love, friendship, and mutual respect. I assumed Blake and I would have a marriage built on these same things.

My folks also modeled a pretty traditional marriage in terms of their roles. My father was the primary breadwinner, spending his days at the office. At home, Dad paid bills and balanced the checkbook; he worked in the yard and built or fixed things. Mom worked part time or not at all, was the main caregiver for my younger brother and me, and took care of most of the cooking and cleaning. Evaluating it now, I guess watching my parents gave me a picture of marriage as a loving, equal, and committed partner-ship, in which each person has distinct roles, but both gain a great love and a teammate to tackle life with.

As a very small child, I distinctly recall lying in bed at night, listening to my mom and dad in their own room, quietly chatting or laughing. I remember, even at that young age, thinking how nice it must be to have a friend to talk with before falling asleep every night. I looked forward to the day when I'd have that too. As far as I could see, everything would be twice as good when I got married because there would be two of us contributing to a new life, creating it together.

Emotionally, I expected that marriage would give me someone to lean on; someone to laugh, talk, and go on dates with; someone to share birth-days, anniversaries, and Valentine's Days with. Ultimately I wanted some-one with whom I could start a family and grow old, someone who could be a loving protector and provider.

Practically speaking, I thought marriage would make life easier because all work and responsibilities would be shared equally. I assumed that with two of us working, splitting household chores, sharing finances, and making big decisions, the hard work of being a grown-up would ease up a little. I imagined my husband and me working as a team, complementing each other, challenging each other, and being better together than we were individually.

With Blake's illness, the whole notion of marriage making things easier, the idea that someone would always be there for me, the dream of an eternally equal partnership all started to dissolve. I didn't know if Blake would make it to our second anniversary, let alone our twentieth. I had to make decisions for both of us and be physically, mentally, and emotionally strong—for two. Oftentimes, I had to carry more than what I thought was my "fair share" of responsibility in our marriage. On our wedding day, I wholeheartedly pledged to love Blake "in sickness and in health," having no idea how quickly that would be tested or what it would actually look like! I wanted more than anything to keep Blake, to love him faithfully, but I was scared and confused; this wasn't what I imagined marriage would be like.

One of the first lessons I learned through this grueling ordeal is that when you join your life with someone else's, it sometimes means carrying the weight of not just one but two people. Most of us want someone who will be there for us and with us, but we aren't as eager to deal with the suffering that comes with knitting your heart together with another person's, the constant negotiation of roles and responsibilities that comes with marriage, or the reality that it's impossible for things to feel fair 100 percent of the time.

I wasn't prepared to take on all the housework and details of financial management, plus caring for a sick husband and everything that went along with it. I suddenly found myself doing the majority of the work for both of us. I hated thinking of myself when Blake was the one dealing with cancer, but there were so many days my tired, worn-down body urged me to give in to bitterness, deep disappointment, and agonizing loneliness.

Next to loneliness, guilt was probably the most common emotion I struggled with—guilt for feeling resentful, guilt for being too "strong" and wondering if I was doing enough to support Blake emotionally, guilt for feeling disappointed in my husband for something he had no control over, and, most of all, guilt for feeling sorry for myself when I wasn't the sick one.

Thankfully, God provided a lot of support from our church community. Our nearest family members were more than three hundred miles away, so while they came out periodically to help, we really had to rely on our friends and neighbors. They brought meals and made visits, gave gifts and encouragement, prayed for us all the time, and were ready at a moment's notice to do anything we asked. Without them, I don't know how we would have made it through. Still, I spent many nights driving home from the hospital by myself, feeling wasted and burned-out. In these moments, I needed God more than ever before.

How can I ever thank Him for His tender care and provision during this time? He even used things like the premarital counseling Blake and I had received to encourage and uplift me. I remember Him bringing one session in particular back to my mind, a time when Blake and I studied the passage in Ecclesiastes 4 that proclaims, "Two are better than one, because they have a good return for their work: If one falls down, his friend can help him up. . . . If two lie down together, they will keep warm" (verses 9-11, NIV).

I think I understood this part pretty well going into our marriage—it echoed what I thought would be so great about being married in the first place! At the end of that passage, however, and seemingly out of nowhere, the author switched gears and declared, "A cord of three strands is not quickly broken" (verse 12, NIV).

The Lord reminded me of the words the pastor who did our premarital counseling had spoken about this verse: It's God, the "third strand," that truly makes a marriage strong. There were times in our two-year battle when I was incredibly overwhelmed, moments I felt so alone. Truthfully,

I sometimes wondered why I'd ever decided to get married at all. Looking back, I now see that during those times God came alongside me (and Blake, too). Without His grace, extra doses of strength and patience, and "daily bread" to make it through the next twenty-four hours, I don't know how we'd have done it—definitely not in our own strength.

Before Blake's diagnosis, I was fairly confident in my ability to be loyal and caring—after all, he was my husband and I was in love with him; how hard could it be? I was so surprised and humbled when, during my most desperate moments, I just wanted to run away, not because I loved my husband any less, but because I hated the cancer and what it was doing to our marriage. Sometimes I wondered whether we even had a "real" marriage anymore; there were days I felt less like a wife and more like a nurse. During those times, I couldn't do anything but pray that God would help me keep the "in sickness and in health . . . in good times and bad" parts of my vows. I know it was only His strength and grace working through me that helped me persevere. Relying on my own strength, I probably would have given in to despair. Instead, through joy and pain, I've clearly seen that if I trust God with my marriage, He will help me keep my vows. Blake cannot always be there for me, but the Lord can.

I have also learned (and am still learning) deep and freeing lessons about love. How clearly and powerfully He's communicated to me that His sovereign grace often demands sacrifice in return.

Many times during Blake's treatment, when praying, I was reminded of Abraham and Isaac. This troubled me because the tale of Isaac's near sacrifice was one of those incidents in the Bible that I didn't like to think about; truthfully, it always bothered me. Why would God give Abraham the thrill of a much-anticipated son, only to demand—as proof of obedience—that he take that son and put a knife to his throat? And honestly, how could Abraham agree to go through with it? To me, this story presented a pretty sadistic picture: a God I didn't really understand and didn't care to know more about. As Blake and I fought his cancer together, however, our experiences helped me understand this story in a new way.

When Blake was first diagnosed, I tried to control everything. I took copious notes in the doctors' offices, kept a detailed list of his medications, cleaned our apartment obsessively so he wouldn't be exposed to anything that might make him sicker—basically, I acted as if it were entirely up to me to make him well again. Of course, I couldn't keep that pace up forever, and the more I tried, the more tired and angry I got.

I also battled the frustration of not understanding why the Lord would give me a husband, only to let him get cancer so soon into our marriage and maybe even take him away from me altogether. Slowly, however, I began to see that if I was going to act based on what I said I believed about God, I had to let go of control and trust Him to handle the cancer. I needed to acknowledge that, although the Lord gave me Blake, my husband still belonged to Him first and to me only second. God would take care of Blake in His own way, and I was invited to trust that, no matter what that meant, His will was good and perfect (see Romans 12:1-2).

Over time, I began to discern that God wasn't acting sadistically when He asked Abraham to lay Isaac down at the altar. Abraham wasn't crazy for actually obeying the Lord's directive. On Moriah, in an incredibly powerful way, God was reminding Abraham—and us as his descendents—that He was, is, and will always be in control. Through Abraham and Isaac, the Lord also displayed the sacrificial nature of real love: The only way to ensure the good of our most precious gifts is to trust God with them completely. It's definitely a hard thing to do, something I still have to work on. And it's not a fun lesson because it's one we humans only learn with a lot of pain, but I think it helped give me a better understanding of God's love for us, His sacrifice, and His ultimate plan for our lives.

I would never wish on anyone the ordeal of Blake's and my battle against cancer. But I do pray that everyone would experience the kind of life-giving freedom that comes with releasing your expectations to God and allowing Him to remake them according to His plans. If reading our story *can encourage anyone, all praise and glory to the God who is always with me, always there for me. He is my strength and salvation.*

Doubling, Dividing, and Suffering

I don't think anyone goes into marriage dreaming about what beautiful fruit the suffering of marriage will produce in them. On the day I married Jeramy, that honestly had to be the furthest thing from my mind. Like Megan, I imagined sharing life with my beloved, falling asleep in his arms, celebrating holidays and special events, growing old together. Though I might not have articulated it in precisely the same terms as Megan did, I also felt that marriage would provide me with an equal partnership, a teammate, and an infinitely better life. Surely Jeramy and I would prove the old adage irrefutably true — "a good marriage doubles the joy and divides the sorrows of life."

Ten years into the adventure of matrimony, I still believe there is a great deal of truth in that simple saying. But like many marriage maxims, these words can be a bit misleading. Perhaps tacking a qualifier, such as "most of the time" or "in the grand scheme of things," onto the beginning of that statement would render it a bit more generally applicable.

What Megan learned in such extreme circumstances, and what I believe every husband and wife learn on some level, is that "when you join your life with someone else's, it sometimes means carrying the weight of not just one but two people."

Not only does marriage sometimes fail to divide the sorrow of life; now and then it actually doubles it. There are times when being married means enduring pain that would easily overwhelm two, and enduring it not *with* your spouse but *because* your life is joined to his. Marriage brings with it pains and disappointments that might well have been avoided if one stayed single forever.

If pressed, most people would probably concede that all of life is full of ups and downs, laughter and tears. Suffering is part of the human equation, and marriage is no exception to the rule. Why, then, do we so often (and sometimes desperately) try to ignore or suppress this truth?

As a young girl, I remember hearing *The Princess Bride*'s hero, Westley, remark, "Life is pain, Highness. Anyone who says differently is selling something."[1] I chafed at such a notion, full of youthful idealism and confident that if I worked hard enough or had a good enough attitude or maybe prayed the "right" kinds of prayers, a happy and relatively trouble-free life was well within my grasp.

Yet as I grew up, and as the bitterness of suffering spread into different parts of my life, the words of Jesus in John 16:33 made far more sense: "Here on earth you will have many trials and sorrows" (NLT). My Lord didn't pose this business of pain and distress as a possibility but a positive imperative—you *will* have trials and sorrows . . . and many of them, to boot.

Still, I thought marriage would be a refuge, a safe haven from the storms of life. I understand why psychiatrist and author John Levy, a veteran of marriage counseling, once wrote that most complaints about matrimony arise not because it is worse than the rest of life but because it is not *incomparably better*.[2]

When I was single, I believed married life would be far superior to, much easier than, and infinitely more pleasant than singlehood. Perhaps I wasn't quite as naive as I once was, a little girl childishly dismissing Westley's difficult words to Buttercup. Even before I met Jeramy, pain had left its marks on me. I thought I understood that there *would* be trials and sorrow in life. But didn't Jesus also command me to "take heart, because I have overcome the world" (John 16:33, NLT)? Certainly, He did! And as truly life-affirming and world-changing as these words are, I sometimes falsely interpreted them as meaning all of the "good things" in life (and I definitely counted marriage among them) would be *primarily* a business of overcoming. Sure, there would be hard times, but those moments would be in the minority, I believed.

Instead, I discovered marriage is like life itself, a continual process of both wounding and healing, giving and taking away. In his classic work *The Mystery of Marriage*, Mike Mason brilliantly explained this:

> *What is given in marriage is fairly obvious: the love of another human being. What is taken away is perhaps not quite so apparent. . . . If people understood the true depth of self-abnegation that marriage demands, there would perhaps be far fewer weddings. For marriage . . . would be seen not as a way of augmenting one's comfort and security in life, but rather as a way of losing one's life for the sake of Christ. . . . Not only does marriage fail to mitigate the struggles of life, but there is a way in which it actually deepens them, rendering them even more poignant, because more personal. . . . All the pain locked up in two lonely, self-centered lives is no longer hidden or suppressed (as it tends to be everywhere else in life), but rather released, released so that in the hands of love it might be used as the raw material for sanctification. Marriage is a way not to evade suffering, but to suffer purposefully.*[3]

In Blake and Megan's situation, God used a battle with cancer as the raw material for sanctification. Thankfully, not every married couple will have to face chemo and skin-grafting surgery. There is, however, no doubt: *Every* husband and wife will be confronted with afflictions, with distress, with suffering. We can learn from Blake and Megan's marriage because they have been taught a good deal about what sacrificing expectations and surrendering agony into the hands of God actually look like.

So often we hope marriage will help erase the pain in our lives (or at least enable us to avoid it a bit longer). But this mind-set only leaves the anguish "hidden [and] suppressed . . . locked up in two lonely, self-centered lives." Whether we are married or single, God urges us to suffer purposefully, releasing pain into the scarred hands of Love. For singles, suffering purposefully will take on a unique character and tenor. In marriage, it often means confronting the truth that our spouse can*not* and will *not* always be there for us.

Suffering also reminds us that *we* cannot and will not always be there, even for the ones we love most. Blake's lengthy and arduous fight against cancer revealed to Megan just how impossible it was for her to be perfectly loyal and caring. Without God, the promise to love "in sickness and in health" seemed overwhelming. At times, being married to an ailing husband seemed far more painful than pleasant. But as Megan chose, and as any of us choose, to release our suffering into the hands of Love—to trust the only One who *can* and *will* be there for us—we find hope, intimacy with God, and deeper love for one another.

Marriage does not inherently (or immediately) lessen the agony of our battles. But it does provide one way for us to suffer purposefully, to allow pain to reform us more fully in God's image. As Paul wrote to the church in Thessalonica, "All this trouble is a clear sign that God has decided to make you fit for the kingdom. You're suffering now, but . . . Grace is behind and through all of this, our God giving himself freely, the Master, Jesus Christ, giving himself freely" (2 Thessalonians 1:5-6,12).

In suffering, the Lord of love draws near, often *so* near that He feels too close for comfort. One might wish that He didn't love us quite so fiercely, that His mercies were not quite so severe. But in this example of powerfully present love He urges us to follow: pressing in ever nearer, giving ourselves freely as Jesus Christ gave Himself for us, identifying completely with the suffering of our beloved, regardless of the messiness. In doing so, we become more like God, fit for His kingdom, ready for His work.

Many of us dream of or begin marriage expecting that we'll always have someone to share life with, someone we'll be able to scale the mountains and navigate the valleys with, someone who will always be there for us. Suffering initially appears to undermine these assumptions at their core. Ultimately, however, the pain we endure enables us to perceive more clearly that we *do* have someone to share life with, someone who will *always* be there for us. It's just not an earthly spouse.

Instead, the Someone who will walk through the valley of the shadow of death with us (see Psalm 23:4), the Someone who will never leave or fail us (see Deuteronomy 31:6) is the same God who proclaims, "You will call me 'my husband' instead of 'my master.' I will make you my wife forever, showing you righteousness and justice, unfailing love and compassion" (Hosea 2:16,19, NLT).

As I've pointed out before—and will again and again—we cannot expect from a spouse what only God can give. God alone is present and faithful . . . *forever*. We don't know how long we'll have our spouse, or whether we'll get married in the first place. We can't predict what sufferings may cross our path (though we can be sure that trials and troubles will come). And we may know these things intellectually, but that's not enough. We must believe with our hearts and live out the truth that only God can share every aspect of life with us, always be there for us.

Whether we are married or single, suffering teaches us this truth powerfully and painfully. But, as we've seen, in the lessons and learning we can find purpose, meaning, and ultimate redemption. Release your pain into the hands of God, and you will find His faithful love truly does endure forever (see Psalm 136). You will also find you have more balanced expectations for your earthly loved ones.

In Daily Practice . . .

Through suffering, people can begin to develop a more balanced view of how much a spouse can be there for them and share their life. And, practically speaking, this makes the constant negotiation of roles and responsibilities, decisions and surrenders in marriage easier to deal with. As Megan observed, it's impossible for marriage to feel fair 100 percent of the time. A healthy, Christ-focused mind-set enables spouses to deal with threats to their sense of justice and equality. To close this chapter, let's consider how these truths intersect with our day-to-day routines.

Before we get married, we sometimes assume that the mundane details of life will be far more bearable as long as we have someone to face them with. But what if your spouse makes getting the oil changed or dealing with taxes seem *more* complicated and *more* tedious? What happens when, as Megan and Blake experienced, being married means dealing with twice as many unexciting tasks because your spouse cannot tackle them? What if your spouse baldly refuses to face them?

Prior to marrying, many people also expect that spouses automatically share the same desires and do the same things (or at least want to). I love what a newlywed friend, Erin, recently confessed to me:

> *I don't know what made me think I'd marry someone who loved shopping all the time (especially for shoes), or someone who loved watching girly movies, or someone who only liked eating at the restaurants I love, or someone who wanted me to be the dictator of his every waking move. Apparently, I wanted to marry my shadow! . . . I never stopped to think that I may have to do something he loves to do. Duh!*

I can't tell you how many people have assumed they would "marry their shadow," waltzing seamlessly from the single life into a perfectly shared marital union.

There's also an expectation, particularly among women, that spouses should listen to and be interested in whatever the other wants or needs to talk about. Singles may dream about how great it would be to share the story of their day, their joys and triumphs, the details of their web surfing and text messaging with someone else every night. But many spouses find their partners resistant to sharing or ill-equipped to share life in the way they envisioned. When expectations aren't met regarding the division of labor, whose preferences and desires are indulged, and how well communication is reciprocated, bitterness and the beginnings of division can creep in.

In response to this, some couples start to build separate lives, eventually staking their ground and drawing lines between "his life" and "her life." Instead of focusing on a shared life together, these husbands and wives allow assumptions to drive them to detachment and withdrawal.

Other couples try to resolve tensions created from differing expectations by dividing *everything* in their marriage right down the middle, 50/50 so to speak. One husband and wife I know actually take this principle to a financial extreme: They go out for ice cream and each pays half, on the dot; they split every gift, every expenditure with exacting equality. Here's the problem, though: For all their efforts toward loving and equal sharing, this couple seems disconnected and confused, almost as much as the husbands and wives who mean-spiritedly separate their lives.

Conceptually, meeting your spouse halfway may sound like the perfect solution to unmet expectations. And why not rotate who gets to choose the Friday night movie rental or the post-church restaurant, if that will mean your desire gets met 50 percent of the time? After all, isn't marriage about compromise?

Yes, it is. But trying to strike a perfect 50/50 balance may not be the answer to your unfulfilled expectations. Indeed, at the very beginning of their book *Starting Your Marriage Right,* FamilyLife mentors Dennis and Barbara Rainey offered some great wisdom about trying to live by the "50/50 Plan." According to the Raineys, there's a big weakness in this supposed resolution for marital imbalance: "It is impossible to determine if your mate has met you halfway." And because most couples can't agree on where halfway is, "each is left to scrutinize the other's performance from a jaded, often selfish perspective."[4]

The only cure for feeling like things are unfair in marriage (and believe me, there will be *many* of these times) is committing once again to God's plan for marriage, which is to give your all, at all times. The Raineys aptly called this the "100/100 Plan."

Marriage requires 100 percent effort from each spouse, whether the matter in question is bearing responsibility for daily life, compromising on what to do or where to go, being willing to communicate in a different way, or something else altogether.

In the 100/100 Plan, each spouse chooses to live by the promise "I will do what I can to love you without demanding an equal amount in return."[5] Essentially, this is what the marriage vows compel people to promise. But because of the almost-too-familiar wording of those promises (as well as the once-and-for-all way in which couples declare them at the altar), people sometimes neglect the practical application of these principles in everyday matters.

There *are* times when having Jeramy with me at the DMV makes the whole ordeal seem far less excruciating. There are times he watches ridiculously girly movies with me or listens to me go on and on about some issue he'd probably never choose to think about if not married to me (the topic of eyebrow waxing comes to mind). There are moments that each of my assumptions and expectations is fulfilled and satisfied. But then there are times I've been wounded by his disinterest, my own selfish desire, or the inevitable blocks that come in our communication.

Because our sinful natures haven't been sanctified perfectly, I'm not always 100 percent committed to loving Jeramy, nor is he always 100 percent committed to loving me. But this is what we long for. And this is what relying on God (not each other) for eternal faithfulness, understanding, and love enables us to strive toward.

If singles and couples could recognize that a spouse will not always be there for them, that being married won't always make daily life more bearable (or even mean that they'll have a date every Valentine's Day), perhaps they'd be better able to trust and share life with God, the only One who *is* and *will always be* there. His is the enduring security, hope, and companionship that all of us — married or single — actually seek. I pray that each of us will grow better able to discern and live this out, thereby taking pressure off our spouse or our desire for one.

Pressing On . . .

1. What did you think of Megan's description of marriage as "a team effort [with] shared responsibilities, a lot of love, friendship, and mutual respect"? Like me, have you ever imagined marriage as "a refuge, a safe haven from the storms of life"? Are some aspects of these expectations suitable and healthy (reread Ecclesiastes 4:9-12 for help)? If so, how might you strike a balance between appropriate assumptions and the difficult truth this chapter explored — that a spouse cannot always be there for you?

2. In his book *The Biblical View of Sex and Marriage,* Dr. Otto Piper described marriage as "a reciprocal willingness of two persons to assume responsibility for each other."[6] How does this picture fit with the lesson Megan learned — "When you join your life with

someone else's, it sometimes means carrying the weight of not just one but two people"? What do you find most challenging about this truth?

3. Take some time to process how much you do/did expect a spouse to meet daily needs — to be with you in facing mundane responsibilities, to partake in the things you love, to share the story of your day with, and to communicate with you on a reciprocal level. How has this assumption affected your day-to-day life — through particular experiences, conversations, and disappointments — whether in dating, marriage, or even your dreams about them?

4. How does learning to trust in and lean on God, the only One who will always be there for us, take pressure off our spouse or our desire for one? Read Psalm 136. What does the refrain teach about God's love? How might you apply this to the ideas this chapter exposited?

5. I've always found the first two verses of 1 Peter 4 particularly challenging. Read the following and discuss or journal about one of the lessons suffering can teach us:

> *Since Jesus went through everything you're going through and more, learn to think like him. Think of your sufferings as a weaning from that old sinful habit of always expecting to get your own way. Then you'll be able to live out your days free to pursue what God wants instead of being tyrannized by what you want.*

FIVE

I Won't Have to Worry About Money

ONE BLESSED—AND blasted—truth of marriage is this: Knitting your life together in the most intimate way possible for humans reveals and magnifies your issues . . . the ones you battle against and the ones you try hard to ignore. Oftentimes, marriage brings to light concerns and problems you didn't even know you had.

Such was the case with me and money.

Before I met Jeramy, I really had no clue how deep my confusion and anxiety about money went. I knew that I was an almost obsessively frugal spender and that I had pretty strong opinions about what things were and were not worth buying. But I married young, and, unlike some of my peers, I didn't have much experience dealing with money in the "real world." Even if I had, I'm not sure that years of paying rent or creating budgets could have prepared me for what marriage revealed about the state of my heart.

How fearful I was! How concerned about provision and the future! How hard I believed I had to work, controlling and manipulating the numbers, always hoping that I would *finally* feel safe and secure.

But I'm getting ahead of myself. Let me go back and explain a little about how I got there.

My father is a film and television composer, a brilliant and self-employed musician. Over the years, Dad sometimes hired Mom to copy scores for him, thereby keeping a bit of the project budget for a particular movie or TV episode in the family. But my mother's primary work was raising me and my three siblings. We lived off the income—advances and royalties—that Dad procured.

Though I now recognize my understanding was severely limited, here's how I viewed my family's financial situation growing up: While my friends' fathers worked in offices, got paid on the first of the month (and/or the fifteenth), and could count on how much they'd have for summer vacations or Christmas presents, my dad got paid in lump sums and unpredictable quarterly statements. Whatever money came in had to last us for months, and, as artists have experienced for centuries, my dad's income often rose and fell in a "feast or famine" cycle.

I remember feeling so grown up when, during a unit on money in fifth grade, I described our family's finances in those terms—feast or famine. Most likely, I picked this phrase up by listening to my parents or someone else; my teachers, however, thought me perceptive and precocious. Apparently, I talked about money matters more maturely than some of my eleven-year-old peers. But for all my ability to rationally discuss the perceived instability of my dad's earnings, I had *no idea* how profoundly the uncertainty of my family's finances actually poisoned my thinking.

Though our family never went without, I lived with an almost constant fear that "this time" (or pretty soon, or in "the future"), we wouldn't have enough. I overheard conversations about money—some hushed, some dramatically overheated—between my parents. Phrases such as "we're fine now, but just wait until the other shoe drops" stuck with me, and a pit-of-my-stomach anxiety would swell deep inside.

None of these feelings made sense in light of reality. My dad did extraordinarily well for a self-employed musician. To any outside observer, our living situation would have appeared as it was . . . incredibly blessed. But when it came to *feelings* about money and provision, somehow these tools of logic, reason, and wisdom for clear thinking summarily deserted me (or, more realistically, I them).

As I grew older and attempted to manage unruly emotions, I did what came naturally: I tried to control things. I always was a bit of a control freak, but when it came to handling money, my nearly neurotic tendencies kicked into overdrive. Somehow, working hard and keeping things in order held my gnawing sense of insecurity and anxiety at bay. And people actually applauded me for the scrupulously careful accounts I kept, the way I scrimped when so many my age spent recklessly and regularly. Perhaps such encouragement and praise kept me from recognizing how imbalanced my views of money truly were.

For one thing, though I claimed God as the most important Person in my life, I rarely invited Him into the details of my financial dealings. Not that I consciously sought to exclude the Lord, I just (mistakenly and a bit arrogantly) figured the responsibility ultimately fell on me. I had to take care of things . . . or else.

If you would've asked me, even back then, I probably could have explained in a cognitive sort of way that the Lord controls all money; everything belongs to Him. And for a long time, I conveniently left things on that general, doesn't-require-much-of-me level. As I matured in faith and started making more money of my own, I began to tithe monthly, supporting the church or missionaries. But giving, too, I meticulously took charge of, never allowing myself to imagine that God might want to take the financial reins, the controls I held so tightly.

Almost immediately after Jeramy and I joined our lives and accounts, the thin guise covering my financial insecurity blew off entirely. Without realizing how crazy it seemed, I would hug my husband at the door and rifle through his pockets, looking to see if he had any receipts. I now know how insane this behavior is, but at the time it seemed perfectly normal to me. In fact, I used to get angry with Jeramy when he became defensive or frustrated. Didn't he know I was trying to protect us from financial ruin?

It's sad for me to acknowledge, but I could fill several pages with similar tales of my controlling (and often bizarre) attitudes and actions. And it didn't help that neither Jeramy nor I expected the strain monetary concerns could place on our marriage. When we talked about money during our premarital counseling, when we took those (usually very helpful, but definitely not in this case) personality tests, our priorities and ideals seemed to line up with textbook perfection. In principle, we both wanted to honor God; we both valued saving over spending. What could go wrong?

A big part of our problem centered on the disconnect between my head and heart. I could talk a good talk, but what I claimed to believe about God's financial sovereignty didn't translate into practical action. Instead, and rather unwittingly, I allowed multifaceted expectations about money and provision to take root in me. These distorted beliefs cropped up in a myriad of ways.

Because I accepted the experiences and emotions of my childhood as indisputably true, they powerfully dictated my adult perspectives. And, because I had very little concept of a "steady paycheck," of what receiving the same amount once or twice a month would look like, I found it extremely difficult to believe that Jeramy and I would have enough. Ironically and simultaneously, I clung to the assumption that marriage should give me a sense of greater financial security and stability. Though I never articulated it, I expected Jeramy—and the resources he provided—to settle the unrest in my heart. Instead, tensions mounted exponentially.

Oh, how I fought with him about money. (I'm sure you can imagine some of our battles, in light of my confession about going through Jeramy's pockets!) And though my husband certainly wasn't—still isn't—perfect when it comes to viewing and handling money, God truly has used him to help refine my understanding of finances.

One of Jer's life verses is Matthew 6:33, the famous "seek ye first" passage. What I didn't realize before I met Jeramy is how *practical* this verse can be. I love how *The Living Bible* brings Jesus' oft-quoted (but rather less frequently lived-out) words to life:

> *So don't worry at all about having enough food and clothing. Why be like the heathen? For they take pride in all these things and are deeply concerned about them. But your heavenly Father already knows perfectly well that you need them, and he will give them to you if you give him first place in your life and live as he wants you to. (Matthew 6:31-33)*

Jeramy lived in such a way, dealt with money in such a way, that these words made new and complete sense to me. Through my husband, I saw Christ's truth take on real-world flesh and bone. Jeramy did not serve money but used it to serve the Master. I never realized so clearly how I had allowed money to master and control me.

Because I didn't consider myself particularly materialistic or eager to make money, I failed to apply some of the Bible's most pointed passages about money to myself. I sort of skimmed over the whole "you cannot serve both God and Money" bit (Luke 16:13, NIV; Matthew 6:24, NIV).

The sometimes maddeningly intimate, life-on-life sharpening of marriage, however, helped me acknowledge that you can serve money in more ways than just by loving it. Giving finances too much attention—through fear or anxiety—can also squarely place you in money's service.

I didn't expect marriage to uncover such toxic misconceptions within me. And even if I could have identified any of my erroneous beliefs before marrying Jeramy, I may have naively assumed they wouldn't seriously affect our relationship. Like many singles and newly married people, I didn't understand the essential importance of thoroughly analyzing my perspectives on money or evaluating how well (or poorly!) they aligned with God's.

So many of us go through life dealing with money but never really *thinking* about it. Buying and borrowing, saving and selling, investing and indulging—our financial habits become such a part of the fabric of our lives that we rarely take stock of what we believe. Perhaps we don't genuinely want to—it might mean change, repentance, conviction.

Yet in my experience, God consistently brings monetary issues back to hearts earnestly seeking Him. Whether we struggle with insecurity or overspending (or both, alternately), there is always something new—and life-changing!—we can learn about dealing with resources in *His* ways, with *His* perspective. Time and again, the Lord weaves lessons about money into my life, always revealing more of Himself, mercifully illuminating the dark and neglected corners of my mind. How I wish I'd given Him greater room to start transforming me before I married Jeramy.

Perhaps in recounting the fits and starts of my own journey, in sharing some of what God has taught me, I might help others appraise their attitudes, expectations, and assumptions about marriage and money. With God's help, maybe they—maybe you—will start the first (or fifth, or fifteenth) year of matrimony in a better place than I did.

Deeper Than Our Pockets

I know the particulars of my story aren't typical, but the experience of getting into marriage and discovering all kinds of financial stresses genuinely *is*. Almost every couple battles financial concerns of one kind or another.

A friend and I just recently shared a laugh about how hard managing money was in the first years of our marriages. Her husband would send her to the grocery store with what they could afford — only twenty dollars for a week's supplies (and this was not too long ago). She told me she'd stand there, wanting to cry, not seeing how in the world she could make things work, not knowing how to communicate about money, not understanding what it would take to run a household in a God-honoring way. We can laugh about it now, but at the beginning of a marriage, such financial anxieties can feel suffocating and consuming.

In fact, professional counselors report that monetary concerns destroy more marriages than any other issue.[1] Over the first few years of my own married life, the reason became *vividly* clear: To every individual, money represents something more than simple dollars and cents. For some, like me, finances intertwine with concerns about safety, protection, and the future.

For others, issues of personal preference and desire come to the forefront. They expect that marriage will give them what they long for — whether that be a prosperous living, the ability to stop working and stay home, or the proverbial American dream — you know, a couple of children, a nice SUV, a comfortable home, and the white picket fence to surround it.

Many Christian women equate marriage with financial security and freedom. I recall talking with one girl who couldn't wait to get married, quit her job, and stay home with the kids. Not only did this reveal her unchallenged assumption that being married would allow her to stop working; it also indicated another layer of expectation, namely that marriage and a family always go together.

I want to be clear: I absolutely sympathized with this young woman. I entertained similar thoughts before I met Jeramy. When dealing with car problems or housing concerns, I also imagined, "When I get married, things will be easier; I'll have someone to help bear the burden of these expenses." Most of the time, my thoughts had less to do with actual money and more to do with the deepest hopes, fears, and dreams of my heart.

Bottom line, money matters reach far deeper than our pockets and purses; they touch the very core of our beliefs about work, security, and being taken care of, provided for, and cherished.

Thankfully, our Lord understands this. Why else would the Bible's Author and Editor devote twice as many verses to finances as to faith and prayer combined? Why else would Jesus say more about money than both heaven and hell? Why, if He did not know the profound ways in which financial issues influence us, would Jesus spend more time discussing how we view and handle money than any one other thing?[2]

How we think about and deal with money indicates *far more* than our level of fiscal responsibility. Indeed, as pastor and author Randy Alcorn boldly proclaimed, "Our perspective on and handling of money is a litmus test of our true character . . . an index of our spiritual life. Our stewardship of money tells a deep and consequential story." Indeed, "if Christ is not Lord over a person's money and possessions, then he is simply not that person's Lord."[3]

If you're anything like me, Alcorn's words border on profoundly disturbing. It's not that I don't believe his claim; I *absolutely* do. Here's the problem, though: It can be incredibly difficult to write a God-honoring "story" with our financial decisions—especially when everything around us screams, "Money will make you happy!" "Money will give you freedom!" "Money is the answer to your concerns and anxieties!"

What story are you currently telling through your stewardship of money? If a clinician had only the evidence of how you view and deal with finances to evaluate, what might the results of such a litmus test of your character be? What about the index of your spiritual life?

I know there's nothing comfortable about asking, let alone attempting to answer, such questions. But what if pressing into this uneasy territory could help us authentically confront our expectations about money? Would it be worth it?

With complete confidence and a desire to journey with you, let me answer that last question: Definitely! I've walked down this road for some time, and though the adventure isn't always easy, Jesus *always* walks with me. And I would rather be with Him on the high road than endlessly trying to find peace elsewhere.

I've already admitted some of the ways money mastered and controlled me as a single and young married. Let me tell you now that as God continually refines me, He's gloriously equipping me, transforming me from the inside out. I'm far from perfect when it comes to viewing or handling finances, but—perhaps because of my upbringing, perhaps because of my analytic nature, perhaps because of some combination of forces that I could never put into words—I have thought, prayed, and read a great deal more about money than I ever intended to. The difference in my life is tangible, and though you may have far less (or a bit more) to plow through than I did, you can experience God's redemptive power by purposefully looking at how you think about and deal with money.

Undoubtedly, how we perceive finances and how we act with regard to them are matters of great importance. Whether you stay single or get married, working through the following prevalent misconceptions about money will make a lasting difference. So let's dive in together, asking God to direct and change us.

What's Your Starting Point?

Make even a quick perusal of the resources available for Christians wishing to set or accomplish financial goals, and you'll find a virtually endless number of practical tips. Websites, DVDs, conferences, and books all claim to help believers establish sound strategies for handling money—both now and in the future.

Truly, such resources can be a great asset to the body of Christ. But any financial counsel, even the most practical of advice, serves its purpose only if the objectives people have in sight are biblically based and Christ-centered. For some of us, learning the latest techniques for mastering money could actually be akin to swabbing the decks of the *Titanic*.

Sure, it often seems far easier, not to mention more pragmatic, to focus on maintaining our ship (implementing sensible monetary strategies) rather than evaluating the ultimate course we've chosen (which we do by carefully considering what we think about money). But here's the thing: When your boat's headed for an iceberg, it does little good to polish the silver or clean the deck chairs. Just so, when you've started your financial journey on a faulty course, with mistaken navigational information and a proverbial iceberg in the middle of your path, it's pointless to talk about budgets, investments, and the like. In order to make any sense of the wealth of information available to those of us seeking financial wisdom, we need to start transforming from the right point—our most rudimentary thoughts about how the universe works.

There really are only two ways of looking at money, resources, and how people deal with them. With or without knowing it, people who reject God automatically adopt a *materialistic perspective*. Those surrendered to God can develop a *Christ-centered view*.

Perhaps the word *can* escaped your notice in that last statement. But this small word is crucially significant. For while failing to choose

God inevitably leads down the path of materialism, simply making a decision for Christ does *not* necessarily establish someone, or a married couple, on a God-honoring financial course. Materialism is the default belief system (including monetary arrangement) of a world broken by sin, and sadly, many who claim fellowship with Christ live out of beliefs marred by materialistic thinking.

Before we continue on this line, it's imperative that we break for a moment and define our terms. The words *materialism* and *materialistic* connote very specific things to some people. Images of spoiled kids, always lusting after the next thing they *have* to have, may come to mind. A corporate executive consumed with appearances, driving a German sports car, wearing designer suits, and wanting nothing more than to "get rich" may define your understanding of materialistic. Or the fashion handbag–carrying, shopping-obsessed, glorified-in-song "Material Girl" may represent your perception of materialism at its height.

Certainly, these images speak a great deal about what materialism does to people, where it takes them, and how it infects their daily lives. But we sometimes mistakenly believe that materialism is only about things, about people believing that "he who dies with the most toys wins." In truth, that is where materialism *ends,* not where it begins. As Randy Alcorn so brilliantly put it,

> *Materialism does not begin with a wrong view of things; it ends there. It begins with a wrong view of God, which produces a wrong view of man and a wrong view of things. . . . Materialism is an attempt to find meaning in a universe that has been stripped of meaning through the denial of its Creator. This is the heart and soul of materialism—it is not a random form of behavior but the logical conclusion of an incorrect theology.*[4]

For a sinful world, hell-bent on taking God out of the equation, materialism is the natural and inevitable consequence. Quite simply, materialism is a mind-set, a life-defining worldview that claims the material universe is all that exists (and is therefore all that matters).

In order to help us understand how materialism affects our lives and relationships, it's important to get a little historical perspective on the subject. Let's look briefly at how English thinker Thomas Hobbes helped define the materialist worldview. According to Hobbes' systematic philosophy,

> *There is nothing but matter and the motions of material things, both outside our bodies and within them. . . . Good and evil are simply what people desire or dislike, right and wrong are what are permitted or forbidden by law. Human actions arise out of a desire for self-preservation and the laws of nature permit any action reasonably intended for that purpose.*[5]

Sounds strikingly like the relativist thinking of our day, does it not? It may not surprise you to know, then, that this same Thomas Hobbes once profoundly influenced a young nation and its founding fathers. You can't miss Hobbes' social contract and his description of the inalienable rights of "life, liberty, and 'the means of so preserving life as not to be weary of it'" (i.e., happiness) in the U.S. Declaration of Independence and Constitution. The U.S. currency may claim "In God we trust," but many of America's fundamental beliefs come from passionately materialistic sources.

Modern society, too, aggressively campaigns for materialism. Advertising subversively (or, more recently, with blatant obscenity) inundates us with a materialistic perspective. Many people begin the journey of, or toward, marriage with these media-driven ideas firmly entrenched in their thinking. They find it difficult to evaluate how materialism affects them or their relationships. But failing to do so is a recipe for trouble.

Indeed, whether we stay single or get married, in today's day and age we are so continuously bombarded with materialistic images and messages that many of us start to believe the lies we've been told since childhood: This is all there is . . . this is what you *need* . . . no one else is going to take care of you . . . you are the sum of what you have, of what you look like.

Every year, and with their wallets, Americans prove "in what" they trust. (Despite what our dollar bills claim, for most people, it's *not* God.) Americans trust in things. Collectively, we spend billions of dollars to obtain the "right stuff." Children fight over who gets to play with what; marriages break down over strain and desire; friendships fall prey to envy and greed. People sacrifice their integrity and dignity to buy and to hoard . . . and what happens to it all? The cell phone of two years ago ends up in a recycling bin; the original iPod collects dust even as the newer model becomes instantly outdated. The wasted toys, trinkets, and treasures are piled at donation centers or junkyards. All that we own eventually becomes litter, useless and abandoned. Where is materialism then? Screaming at us, "Get more, do more, you *need* more."

Only the voice of Truth and Life can break the suffocating monotony of materialist thinking. Jesus boldly proclaimed, "Beware, and be on your guard against every form of greed; for not even when one has an abundance does his life consist of his possessions" (Luke 12:15, NASB).

Before we get married, or right this instant (especially for those of us who are already married), we can choose to reject the default belief of this world: materialism. In order to live financially God-honoring lives, we must actively choose, sometimes over and over again, to say no to the subversive and polluted thinking that surrounds us.

It's essential to note that rejecting materialism is not merely a matter of saying no to things, though God certainly may work on our hearts in that way. At the core, however, He's calling us to say yes to Him, to His view of the universe. Right thinking about resources and finances organically *follows* right thinking about God and His nature. We cannot begin from the other end of that equation.

Yes, we need to develop a healthy perspective on material things. But that can come only after we reject the "incorrect theology" of materialism, which tells us this life, this stuff, this toy, this _____ (you fill in the blank) is as good as it gets.

As I told you before, I never considered myself a particularly materialistic person. But through the years, I've witnessed the lingering remnants of materialism in my heart, of crooked thinking about God that leads to crooked thinking about things. I may try to convince (even succeed in convincing) myself that I don't need that fancy-label purse or those new CDs, that flat-screen TV or an expensive outfit. But if, deep down, I ever struggle with trusting that God is who He claims to be—provider, protector, preserver—then the claws of materialism still have a grip on me.

And whether I love material things or despise them may not make as much of a difference as I thought. Just as is true with money's mastery, I can succumb to materialism both through affection for and obsessive rejection of things.

The alternative? In daily thoughts and choices, I can focus on who God *really* is.

I don't know where you stand on the materialism front, whether you struggle with wanting everything or suppress desire for anything. I also don't know what God might be calling you to do with the "things" in your life. Here's what I *do* know: What matters most is starting from the right point, beginning the journey with a right view of God. If, either before or in the early stages of marriage, you can develop and live out a correct view of who God is and what He says about money, you will experience far less financial tension than your peers, even those intent on incorporating sound financial planning into their lives. So now that we've evaluated what being materialistic really looks like, let's turn to the kind of provider, protector, and preserver God reveals Himself to be.

Who's Supposed to Do What?

When it comes to money and financial security, everyone trusts in something. The more reliable the object(s) of our confidence, the less we need to worry about, work out, or arrange for ourselves.

As we all know—at least intellectually—no career, investment, or source of income is ultimately trustworthy. It may provide well for a few months, a few years, even a few decades; but because job and stock markets are volatile and uncertain, establishing these things as the central foci of our trust will only produce anxiety.

A bit harder for us to grasp is the truth that no *person* is completely worthy of our financial confidence. We have a tendency to hang a very heavy weight of responsibility on the rather thin wire of our loved ones' provision, whether parents' or spouse's. Most women expect—at least in some measure—to be provided for and cherished. Even those hardened by abandonment and loss often prove this point—bitterness and regret could not consume someone with zero expectation of protection or provision.

One of the great challenges of life, then, is sorting out how much we can trust in a spouse (or ourselves, or our parents) to protect, provide for, and preserve us. This is yet another reason it's absolutely essential to establish—in our minds *and hearts*—the truth of what kind of provider God is.

In Him alone can we completely trust. Only He will never break or betray a confidence. He alone knows all we need. Indeed, through the prophet Isaiah, our Lord declared, "I will provide for [my people's] needs before they ask, and I will help them while they are still asking for help" (Isaiah 65:24, NCV).

No spouse, no loved one of any kind, could provide for us in this way. As devoted as Jeramy is to working, to taking care of me and our daughters, he cannot know everything we need before we ask. Jeramy will never have the resources to meet all our needs. Instead, as the apostle Paul declared, the "same God who takes care of me will supply all your needs from his glorious riches, which have been given to us in Christ Jesus" (Philippians 4:19, NLT). Not only *can* God provide for us—He *will* do it.

Of course, talking about the Lord's glorious provision in this way confuses, even angers, some people. How can anyone claim God provides for all when good people lose their jobs and have to go on welfare, when the "have-nots" of the world significantly outnumber the "haves," when children around the globe starve day after day?

I don't pretend to have perfect answers for these pressing and perplexing questions. But I do know that it was in the land of Moriah (where God called Abraham to sacrifice his son), in a place of confusion and suffering and ultimate redemption, that one of God's names first came into use—*Jehovah Jireh*: the Lord will provide (see Genesis 22:14).

Like Abraham, we cannot always see the end of the story from the beginning. But we can choose to believe, as this great man of faith did, that "God himself will provide" (Genesis 22:8, NIV). Written into the core of our heavenly Father's identity, into His very name, is the truth that *He will provide.* His provision may surprise us (or infuriate us, depending on the state of our heart and circumstances), but it will always come through.[6]

As 1 Thessalonians 5:24 reminds us, "The One who called you is completely dependable. If he said it, he'll do it!" When it comes to provision, we need look no further than our faithful, true, and absolutely able God. On earth, the Lord often gives us others to help protect and care for us, but it is *He* who is ultimately responsible for our preservation.

If we become confused on this point, if we look to our spouse or to our own work to meet our needs (whether legitimate needs like food and clothing or perceived needs that stretch beyond what is required to survive), we will miss our chance to know God's complete provision, His tender care.

Often, and tragically, this is precisely what happens in marriage. We look to our spouses and feel resentful, or at least disappointed, when finances are tight. We look to things and spend more than we make to obtain them. But financial pressures, especially those related to excessive debt, play a major role in more than half of all divorces.[7] Many women trust in their spouses to provide, so much so that when a husband is out of work for nine months or more, studies indicate that four of five marriages dissolve.[8] Of course, not trusting in God's provision is only one piece in the complex jigsaw of provider confusion and divorce. But it is a large piece and one we would do well not to ignore.

Before you marry, or wherever you are right now, you can sort out who's supposed to do what, who's ultimately responsible for your well-being. In whom are you choosing to trust: yourself, your parents, your spouse, or your God? Even if you and/or your spouse make an insane amount of money and you never want for any*thing*, you always go wrong if you trust in worldly provision more than the Lord's. By trusting in *Jehovah Jireh*—the Lord will provide—you will not want, physically or spiritually (see Psalm 23).

With the psalmist, I pray these verses would define our lives: "Whom have I in heaven but You? And besides You, I desire nothing on earth. My flesh and my heart may fail, but God is the strength of my heart and my portion forever" (Psalm 73:25-26, NASB). He is your portion, your more-than-enough. Your flesh will fail; your loved ones will fail; if you have storehouses of goods or piles of money, they, too, will eventually fail you. *Only He* is from everlasting to everlasting.

I realize that actually living in this truth is challenging; I'm in the trenches with you! That's why it's imperative for me to go back to God's Word regularly, allowing Him to remind me what kind of provider He is, how He preserves and protects me. I urge you to do the same and also to make use of some of the great Christian resources listed in the Notes section of this book.[9]

Deciding to live in these truths—that God (not material things) defines the universe, that the Lord will provide, and that He is responsible for our well-being—is the most important and fundamental choice we can make about money. With these views solidly in our hearts, we can turn our attention to some final and practical details regarding money and marriage.

The Greater the Weight . . .

As I mentioned earlier, debt plays a major role in many divorces. Debt also plays a significant part in infinitely more separations, fights, and unrecognized marital tensions. And the sad reality is, in the United States, more couples than not are up to their eyeballs in debt.

Credit cards are maxed out; enormous college loans hover over young families like dark storm clouds. All manner of things—from electronics to furniture, from cars to homes (each too expensive to *really* be afforded)—are justified and purchased with "great deals" on financing and monthly payments. Slowly, and often without recognizing it, people seeking a higher standard of living actually end up sacrificing a higher standard of life.[10]

In 2006, the Department of Labor reported that in 51.8 percent of U.S. families (including those with and without children), both the husband and wife were employed.[11] I realize that in today's world, it sometimes takes two paychecks just to survive. But I wonder how many of these families are working primarily to pay off their debts . . . or to finance their automotive, entertainment, or other lifestyle preferences?

I appreciate the way Randy Alcorn discussed debt in his book *Money, Possessions, and Eternity.* He claimed that one of the strongest arguments against going into certain kinds of debt is that we are *not* like God—omniscient, sovereign, and omnipotent. We neither know, nor can control, all that the future holds. So how, Alcorn asked, can we be sure that we can pay off debts incurred today? Before going into debt, he recommended we ask not only, "Are we mortgaging our family's future to pay for the whims of our present?" but also, "Are we mortgaging God by supposing to commit Him to provide for something(s) He may not even approve of?" [12]

Of course, not all debt is in the same category. Very few people can pay for a car, let alone a home or college education, without financing some or all of the cost. I'm certainly grateful the Word of God neither expressly forbids nor unreservedly condones debt.

Instead, with regard to purchases that will place us in debt, singles and couples can pray, seeking God's direction and listening to His counsel. If God doesn't give you peace about buying a $20,000 car, perhaps it's because a $10,000 or even a $2,000 one would be a better option. You may desire a four- or five-bedroom home, but what does God have to say—not only about what you hope for but also about the practical aspects of this expenditure? Do you think God might have an opinion about how you spend the money He's given you?

Here's what often gets us into trouble: We just *don't ask.* We fail to seek His wisdom (either because we don't want to hear what He has to say and fully intend on doing what we want anyway, or because we mistakenly believe God doesn't care about such things). We recklessly purchase what seems a "good deal"—something we might "miss out on"—because we assume that if God says no now, He will never say yes. This is — quite simply — unsound thinking. He may have you in a less desirable home (or car, or job) right now, but that does not mean you will be there forever. How grateful are you for the provision He *has* given? Is the debt you've incurred straining relationship with your family or with the Lord?

Most of the difficulties married couples face with debt result from discretionary, unnecessary, and impulsive expenditures. The consequences of such debt linger, causing worry and stress, eroding our sense of peace.

Again, the point is not to say no to things or to money or even to all debt; rather, the issue at hand is how we can use money and things to *say yes to God*. Resources and material possessions are neither good nor evil. The attitudes and actions associated with them can be, however. By tying up our resources and making them unavailable for other purposes, unnecessary debt can prevent us from being able to say an unreserved yes to God and His kingdom work.

What if, before we married, or in whatever stage of marriage we might be at, we learned to pray before we spent? What if, instead of impulsively buying and spending, we asked God to supply our desires in His way, on His timeline? What if we became less concerned with attaining the so-called good life and more concerned with how committing the resources God has entrusted to us in a particular way would aid or detract from our devotion to the Lord?

Some years ago, a well-known evangelical pastor published a book titled *Whose Money Is It Anyway?* The answer, of course (as any good Sunday schooler would know to respond), is that all money is God's. But so often we forget this most essential truth.

We also sometimes neglect the truth that one day we will give an account for how we choose to steward *His* money, the resources *He's* given us to use and allocate. Depending on how much thought we've given to our financial beliefs and habits, this future accountability can be either a terrifying or wonderful reality to consider. Which will it be for you?

A Final Word

Before we close, I'd like to note that throughout this chapter, my focus has been on encouraging you to carefully consider how you think about money. The details of how to balance a budget, how to relieve impertinently incurred debt, and other such practical matters have been addressed by others more qualified than I.

As far as what people *believe* and *feel* and *know* about money and resources, however, I have learned both from God's Word and the wisdom of others. I've been glad to share some of them with you over the previous pages. I pray they have challenged you to evaluate your views on financial issues before you marry, or within your marriage relationship.

But this is only the beginning of a journey I hope you will take with the Lord, investigating this very important topic of money and resources. Go forth now in hope and grace, becoming even better equipped to deal with finances according to His plan, confident that in doing so you will be proclaiming a resounding *no* to the default thinking of our day and a wholehearted *yes* to God and His work.

Pressing On . . .

1. What did you think about the definition of materialism presented in this chapter? Do you agree or disagree with the claim, "Materialism is the default belief system (including monetary arrangement) of a world broken by sin, and sadly, many who claim fellowship with Christ live out of beliefs marred by materialistic thinking"? Are you ready to evaluate—courageously and honestly—how materialism most often infiltrates your own life?

2. Take some time to ponder the piercing words of theologian A. W. Tozer:

> *Sin . . . has made [the] very gifts of God a potential source of ruin to the soul. Our woes began when God was forced out of His central shrine and things were allowed to enter. . . . There is within the human heart a tough, fibrous root of fallen life whose nature is to possess, always to possess. It covets things with a deep and fierce passion. The pronouns my and mine look innocent enough in print, but their constant and universal use is significant. They express the real nature of . . . man better than a thousand volumes of theology could do. They are verbal symptoms of our deep disease. The roots of our hearts have grown down into things, and we dare not pull up one rootlet lest we die. Things have become necessary to us, a development never originally intended. God's gifts now take the place of God, and the whole course of nature is upset by the monstrous substitution.*[13]

In what, if any, ways have the roots of your heart grown down into things?

3. How do you currently handle debt? Did the ideas this chapter highlighted encourage you to make any changes to your present situation or financial plan? If so, what step could you take today to start the process? Is there someone you could call to enlist as an accountability partner in this endeavor?

4. Read the following familiar words from Matthew 6, in *The Message* translation. Perhaps the fresh wording will help you apply God's Word and the ideas of this chapter in a new way.

You can't worship two gods at once. Loving one god, you'll end up hating the other. Adoration of one feeds contempt for the other. You can't worship God and Money both.

If you decide for God, living a life of God-worship, it follows that you don't fuss about what's on the table at mealtimes or whether the clothes in your closet are in fashion. There is far more to your life than the food you put in your stomach, more to your outer appearance than the clothes you hang on your body.

What I'm trying to do here is to get you to relax, to not be so preoccupied with getting, so you can respond to God's giving. People who don't know God and the way he works fuss over these things, but you know both God and how he works. Steep your life in God-reality, God-initiative, God-provisions. Don't worry about missing out. You'll find all your everyday human concerns will be met.

Give your entire attention to what God is doing right now, and don't get worked up about what may or may not happen tomorrow. God will help you deal with whatever hard things come up when the time comes. (verses 24-25,31-34)

5. Some people unfortunately turn regular and intentional giving into a matter of grace versus legalism—tithing was an Old Testament requirement, they claim, and believers today should have the option to give cheerfully from their hearts or not at all. I challenge you to read the important (if a bit difficult!) words of Malachi 3:8-12 and 1 Corinthians 16:2 and then evaluate your stand on tithing. Are you ready to ask God, "If I am to develop a Christ-honoring perspective on money, should consistent giving be part of my financial plan?"

SIX

I'll Know What to Do with the Rest of My Life

MORE THAN ALMOST ANYTHING else, human beings long for purpose. We yearn to know that we matter, that our lives count for something, that our existence can somehow make a difference on this spinning globe . . . maybe even in eternity.

Unfortunately, some people believe that getting married will give clear purpose and direction to their lives. Long-standing jokes—like the ones about young women who attend Christian colleges only to obtain their "MRS" degree—attest to this. For a good number of us, at some time or another, marriage seems an answer to the nagging question, "What should I do with my life?" or, more importantly, "What does God want me to do with my life?"

For many, the goals of getting married, having kids, and raising a godly family provide all the answers they want or need for these questions. Even some churches falsely teach that a woman's ultimate purpose is to build a godly heritage through homemaking and child rearing. What, I ask you, does this mean for women who desperately desire to marry but never do? What about the countless couples who battle infertility or those who are turned down for adoption? Did these people somehow miss God's purpose for their lives?

The destructive illogic of such thinking is undeniable. And yet such ideas persist, weaseling their way into the minds and hearts of many. The truth is, whether or not you ever get married, you can develop a biblical view of life-purpose by recognizing that while marriage and family may be part of the plan, they are *not* the sum of it.

For other people, having children is a distant thought, not their present hope for purpose and direction. But the idea that a spouse can give clear shape and substance to life may trip these people up, and in a variety of ways. In fact, when I discussed this chapter with a mentor and an amazing godly woman, Jenni, she confessed that before she married her husband, Jim, they planned to go overseas as missionaries and didn't even talk about kids—ever! Nonetheless, Jenni told me she believed, "When I get married, I'll know what I'm doing with the rest of my life, whether it's following my husband where he goes, starting a business, or going on the mission field with him—whatever."

When I get married, I'll know what to do with the rest of my life . . .

The lure of that lie is almost irresistible. Wouldn't we all like to know what we should do with the rest of our lives? And wouldn't it be great if marriage answered that for us? However, as Jenni has discovered (and many others along with her), *marriage doesn't give you direction or purpose.* Only God can. But before we get into that, I'll let Jenni tell you the rest of her story . . .

Finding the "Me" Jesus Intended
As told by Jenni Key

Jim approached me as I was sitting on the grass in front of Wheeler Hall at UC Berkeley, waiting for a class to begin. His opening line was "Are you on staff with Campus Crusade?" I wasn't, but he had seen me at a Bible study there. We talked for about half an hour, and then he invited me to go get a Coke with him. I said no (remember, waiting for a class). Later, he told me he had skipped a class to talk with me and was a little miffed I wouldn't do the same! Eventually I did agree to share a Coke with him, and over the next couple of months, our relationship became serious relatively quickly.

Before Jim and I got engaged, we mainly spent time with a bunch of friends and didn't do a lot of one-on-one dating—to be honest, there were only about ten dates before Jim asked me to marry him. We met in October, started spending time with each other in January, were engaged April 17, and married seventeen weeks later on August 17.

To prepare myself for marriage, I read whatever books were available, but in the early seventies, there weren't many. I also attended Bill Gothard's Institute in Basic Youth Conflicts—which had some portions on biblical principles for marriage—and went to a few seminars with titles such as "Love, Sex, and Marriage." Even at Christian conferences, however, there wasn't a whole lot offered. Our premarital counseling consisted of two or three short sessions. Compared to what's available nowadays, there was a dearth of information or conversation.

Because I wasn't raised in a Christian home and didn't have a whole lot to contradict my ideas, I was rather idealistic about what marriage would be like. I knew very few Christian married couples, and they made even the "work" of marriage look easy, so I thought, Hey! I get that marriage is work (the seminars and books had consistently made this point), but because I understand that, things should be relatively easy.

In my idealistic mind, I imagined that Jim and I would go on the mission field almost right away . . . that we would jointly serve throughout our marriage and that we would be beacons in whatever neighborhood or culture we found ourselves. I imagined that on a day-to-day basis we would awaken and pray, read Scripture at the breakfast table, have people over for dinner almost every night (practicing biblical hospitality, you know), host small-group studies in our home, and eventually rear children who would be the envy of all.

Unfortunately, there were a few problems with this plan.

When Jim and I got married, I believed our immediate purpose was to go on the mission field with Campus Crusade. At the time, however, Crusade wisely would not allow couples to go overseas until they had been married a year. With this derailing of our immediate plans, Jim got a secular job while we "waited out" those twelve months. We've never left Orange County, and we're coming up on thirty-five years of marriage!

About three years after our wedding, I listened to Jim telling some friends what he was planning to do that weekend; it hit me that he continued to think of himself as "I" in our marriage—that "we" was not his natural pronoun—and that we were in no way on the same page about future plans, either for the weekend or beyond. I thought the "we" of marriage would give me not only purpose but also a shared vision and direction with the man I loved. Listening to Jim talk was pretty sobering and made me feel very lonely.

Sometime later, I remember hearing a woman by the name of Dr. Jean Lush speak for Focus on the Family. She had a wonderful sense of humor and turned out to be a real truth-teller in my life, both through her times on the radio and through her books. I remember—as if it were yesterday—when she said something to this effect: "Does your husband come home from work? Is he sober? Is he faithful? Does he provide for you and the children? Then shut up about all he's not doing or being." Wow. That really hit home. I realized all the expectations I had of Jim—that he would be my best friend, my lover, my confidant, my counselor, my intellectual stimulation, my social connection, my financial provider, my spiritual head, my ministry partner, and on and on. I wanted our marriage to give purpose and shape to my life and our life together.

Yikes! I hadn't bothered to share this huge list of expectations with Jim, but when he failed to live up to my (unspoken) assumptions, I was disappointed in him and mad at God. Surely, I thought, God wants me to find fulfillment in all these ways, and through my husband. Somewhere along the way, though, I figured out, "If Jim fulfilled me in all this, what would draw me to the foot of the cross, to seek out Jesus or turn to Him for anything?"

Hope, however, springs eternal, and my unrealistic expectations died slowly. I began to realize—slowly but certainly—that in many ways I had set up an untenable situation for Jim. If he changed his behavior to suit me, then my attitude was either "Well, it's about time" or "That's fine—but it won't last." He really couldn't win, and that became problematic for both of us.

I wish I could say I learned my lesson once and never erred in that way again, but it was a three-steps-forward, two-steps-back sort of thing. And the tension in our first years of marriage was something I tried to address in any and every way—being loving and kind and silent about any disappointment; reminding or nagging him to change; praying and fasting about it; ignoring behaviors and focusing my attention outside the home—in other words, trying all kinds of approaches on my terms, with my own ways. I wanted so desperately to know what God designed as our "true purpose" and "life direction," but oftentimes I was going about things with my own agenda.

Seven years into our marriage—at the time our first child, Matthew, was born—Jim was working one hundred hours a week. It's a complicated story, but he was actually working two full-time jobs with high hopes for the future: a partnership position in a new company. He would come home from one job around two in the morning and then leave around eight in the morning for the other. He rarely saw Matt, was exhausted all the time, and had little to give either of us emotionally. Our son became my whole world, and my schedule revolved around him. But when Matt was two months old, Jim was fired from what once seemed like such a promising situation. It felt like God, in His grace, hit the "pause" button on our life, all so that we could reassess our purpose and direction.

Even so, it was difficult for me to say anything like, "Hey! What about me? What about my future, my gifts and abilities?" Jim was hurting and uncertain about tomorrow, let alone next year; I didn't feel that I could talk about my hopes and dreams. As God showed Jim new possibilities and he began to try them out, however, all three of us hit a much better stride. Still, that was a very dark time for us. Marriage hadn't given us clear purpose; work hadn't provided the direction and fulfillment we imagined; and before Jim was let go, I was practically single parenting. This was not what I imagined marriage would be like.

By the time our daughter, Emily, came along three years later, our lives were much more ordered, with healthier expectations and some really solid family patterns. I think it felt like a new lease on parenthood for Jim and a second chance at being with a newborn. Thankfully, Matt had been an easy and fun baby as well as a great sidekick for me; Emily, too, really made parenting look easy. I thoroughly enjoyed all my time with them and began to hope that, even after they were reared, there might be something of significance for me to do. I also believed my marriage would survive long enough for that.

I hope this doesn't sound corny, but I'm so grateful that I went through such hard times early in marriage because it kept driving me to Jesus. When

I was at the end of everything, as far as trying to fix things or be a better person or figure out where my life was supposed to be headed, He was there. So many times, I felt like I just had to climb up into the Abba Father's lap and be held by Him.

We had a bunch of friends who bailed early in marriage, and I think one of the main reasons I didn't consider divorce was sheer pride. It seemed like failure. Now I see that if I had divorced Jim, I'd never have two great kids I love, a marriage that is strong and still growing, a husband who has been through so much with me, a ministry to young women and wives, and on and on. James knew what he was saying when he urged us to greet trials—including marital trials—with joy because the testing of our faith has produced endurance (see James 1:2-4).

Now I truly feel that Jim is my greatest fan. He admires my spiritual gifting, and I his. We really see Jesus in each other and are able to rejoice over how we see Him using each of us—sometimes together in ministry, but often in our own spheres. I wouldn't have missed this for anything! At times I was so consumed with not being swallowed up by my roles as a wife, a mother, a teacher, or some other label; I thought I would lose "me" in all that. It turned out just the opposite. I discovered the purpose of my life both in and beyond my life with Jim, but never simply because I was married. I found the "me" Jesus intended. And He continues to do the good work in me that He promises to complete (see Philippians 1:6).

I Only Know That I Am Longing

On February 12, 1944, thirteen-year-old Anne Frank penned the following words in her now-famous diary:

> Today the sun is shining, the sky is deep blue, there is a lovely breeze and I am longing—so longing for everything. To talk, for freedom, to be alone.
>
> And I do so long . . . to cry! I feel as if I am going to burst,

and I know that it would get better with crying, but I can't, I'm restless, I go from room to room, breathe through the crack of a closed window, feel my heart beating, as if it is saying, can't you satisfy my longing at last?

I believe that is spring within me, I feel that spring is awakening, I feel it in my whole body and soul. It is an effort to behave normally. I feel utterly confused. I don't know what to read, what to write, what to do, I only know that I am longing.[1]

Within all of us, at the deepest center of who we are, an arresting tension lingers—an aching, a yearning that is profound and unquenchable. Most of the time, like Anne, we cannot name or focus it. Try as we might, we cannot pinpoint it with lucid description. We only know that we are longing, restless, ready to burst. It is an effort to behave normally. We are dying for *meaning,* for *purpose,* for *direction.*

And so many people try to extinguish—or, at the very least, dampen—the restless fire within by getting married. Indeed, Christian psychologists and relationship experts Drs. Les and Leslie Parrott estimated that "most people expect marriage to quench [this] soulful longing, and it often does for a time. But for many, the deep, restless aching echoes again."[2]

In some ways, Jenni sought direction and purpose in marrying Jim, hoping that their life together would give shape to her future. She envisioned them serving God with purpose and passion . . . *together.* She imagined that, somewhere down the road, they would have children and raise them in godliness . . . *together.* Instead, the deep and restless aching of unfulfilled expectations echoed through the lonely weeks when she realized they wouldn't be going on the mission field immediately, when Jim worked one hundred hours a week, when the purpose and direction of her life didn't seem clear or concrete.

Like many of the couples she and Jim knew, Jenni could have thrown in the towel—marriage isn't what it's cracked up to be or what I dreamed of, so why should I stick around? How I praise God that she didn't! As I mentioned, Jenni has been a mentor of mine. And much of the wisdom she's passed on to me, as well as to a host of other young women, was hard-earned during the times when purpose, direction, and meaning *weren't* made clear through her marriage or having children.

Jenni clung to the promises of hope and assurance that her Abba Father offered. And she's been blessed with joy on the other side. Her marriage is stronger than ever, and the way God has used her life in innumerable ways, and on many different levels, is truly remarkable. Hers is the kind of marriage many would consider a "happily ever after," yet Jim and Jenni did not come to this point without significant suffering; they also don't consider their story finished yet. People are desperately aching for a happy ending, for clear vision about the future, but so many are looking in all the wrong places, expecting, as Jenni once did, that marriage itself will somehow answer life's most pressing questions.

If we are to find direction and meaning for our lives, we must do so beyond marriage and beyond having a family. God can and may use these things to shape and change you, but they are not the sum of your purpose here on earth. And this, my friend, is extraordinarily good news! For if marriage alone was to give our lives shape and depth, we'd be in a pretty sorry situation. The mingling of sorrow and love that comes with matrimony is not the "happily ever after" most of us pictured.

But if we look to God for meaning, purpose, and direction, there *can be* a happy ending to each of our tales. Our lives can both begin and end with the victory of the cross. As Psalm 37:37 proclaims, "The good man—the blameless, the upright, the man of peace—he has a wonderful future ahead of him. For him there is a happy ending" (TLB). Why? Because not even death can vanquish the power of Christ's sacrifice, the force of His love.

This is certainly not to say that everything in your life will be rosy. God's purpose and plan for you may include tribulations that, were He to reveal them to you beforehand, might make you want to turn tail and run. But His promise is this: Sorrow will remain only for a season. "Then he turn[s] my sorrow into joy! He [takes] away my clothes of mourning and clothe[s] me with joy" (Psalm 30:11, TLB). Sorrow into joy, mourning into dancing . . . only *He* can do this.

The cynical and ironic world would like you to believe that happy endings are only for fairy tales and children. Blind faith, they call it—or something much worse. Our belief in a happy ending is *not* unrealistic optimism. Trusting in His promise of victory is not "blind faith"; it's staking your life on the truth, and that does and will *last*. As Nicole Johnson wrote, "If our belief is not grounded in truth, it will never sustain us. Enthusiasm will never stand the strain of suffering; only the deeper belief and commitment that we are here for God and his purposes can do this."[3]

We know the incarnated Truth—Jesus—and He has called us according to His purpose. Further, "we know that God causes everything to work together for the good of those who love God and are called according to his purpose for them" (Romans 8:28, NLT). This can sustain us; this can stand the strain of suffering; these are words to build your life on.

Marriage cannot give you the firm foundation of meaning and purpose that you are looking for. Only God can do that. (Do you see the recurring theme of this throughout our journey?) Only He is able, and, honestly, only He is willing. We'd like to imagine that our spouses would sacrifice everything to help us become the people we were created to be. But only God has the long-suffering love that actually makes this possible.

If we are to find true meaning and purpose for our lives, we must first and always go to God for direction. We cannot look to marriage or to child rearing or to anything associated with them. I include "anything associated" because we humans often become deceived and can place even peripherally important things — such as, but certainly not limited to, "healthy communication with my spouse" or "our child's education" — on the throne of our lives. We must only and always look to the Source, to the Lord Himself.

But if we are to turn to God, we must know something of His character and commitment to us. I'd like to take a couple of moments and look at *why* we can — and truly must — trust the restless aching of our hearts for purpose and direction to Him alone.

What Characterizes the God You Serve?

When I attended college, a popular group on campus urged people to surrender their hearts to God because He "has a wonderful plan for each life." Now, I want to make immediately clear that I agree with this statement. I believe it to be biblical and true. Nevertheless, there's a problem with such an assertion: Very few people *actually live* as if it's true.

Why? Why do so many of us claim that we believe God is loving and just, yet go on living as if He's about to capriciously pull the rug out from under our lives? Why do we parrot verses like Jeremiah 29:11 — "'For I know the plans I have for you,' says the LORD. 'They are plans for good and not for disaster, to give you a future and a hope'" (NLT) — all the while running our lives as if God doesn't really have our best in mind?

Certainly, part of the problem stems from a society that has (often willfully) misunderstood the Lord's character. Postmodern authors like international best seller Paulo Coelho articulate the accusing mistrust many people harbor toward God. In his gripping yet tragic novel *Veronika Decides to Die,* Coelho wrote,

> *[Jehovah] devised a rule ["of the tree of the knowledge of good and evil thou shalt not eat"] and then found a way of persuading someone to break it, merely in order to invent punishment. . . . He set a trap, perhaps because he, Almighty God, was . . . bored with everything going so smoothly: If Eve had not eaten the apple, nothing of any interest would have happened in the last few billion years.*[4]

What a disastrous view of the Lord! How insidiously such lies have wormed their way into our thoughts and beliefs. So many people—and certainly not limited to self-proclaimed atheists—accuse God of cruelty or neglect with regard to His creation: If He hadn't put the forbidden fruit there and pointed it out, none of this (sin, shame, pain) would have happened. What could He possibly have intended by setting humans up for near-immediate failure? Was this His purpose and plan for us all along?

Oftentimes, such ideas lie buried in Christians' hearts, beneath years of trying to convince themselves otherwise. Sometimes those who want to believe God is who He claims to be, those who yearn to believe in His sovereign grace and mercy, still find themselves restless and afraid, wondering if the Lord could possibly have a purpose in all the suffering mankind faces. Does He really have plans to give *me* hope and a future?

If we do not squarely face the toxic lies circulated about God, replacing them with biblical truth and the experience of personal intimacy with Him, we will never discover the meaning and purpose we're searching for. Without answering the question "What kind of God do I serve?" we cannot determine the point of our lives, blended as they are with joy and sorrow. We have to *live* and *lean into* the truth. His

Word really is "full of living power . . . sharper than the sharpest knife, cutting deep into our innermost thoughts and desires . . . expos[ing] us for what we really are" (Hebrews 4:12, NLT).

A phrase that helps me do this comes from 1 Timothy 6:15—God "is the blessed and only Sovereign" (NASB). Bible translator J. B. Phillips rendered this "the blessed controller of all things." These words help me remember that not only does God command all things (see Isaiah 45:12), not only does He hold everything under His authority (see Colossians 2:10), but He is both *blessed* and *exclusive* in this power. In other words, He directs the world with perfect goodness and flawless ability.

If I truly believe that God is the blessed and only Sovereign, trusting Him with my future and accepting that His purposes for me are good become much easier. I don't need to fight against a good and exclusive Ruler who not only has my best interest in mind but actually holds the power to make it happen.

This doesn't mean that I (or you) will never feel confused or disheartened by the pain of living in a broken world; we often may. But staking our lives on words like these from the prophet Isaiah—"I will wait for the Lord to help us, though he is hiding now. My only hope is in him" (Isaiah 8:17, TLB)—can make all the difference. These words speak of a decision to trust, a determined hope, even when heaven falls silent.

If Jesus did nothing for any of us after dying on Calvary's cross, His sacrifice would be enough to prove for all eternity that He will do whatever it takes to give us life, hope, love. And yet He continues—daily!—to orchestrate so much for us. Our very breath comes as a gift of His grace (see Acts 17:28).

As we begin to stake our lives on the truths that God actually is who He claims to be and that His purposes for us are genuinely good, we find the restless desire within us quieting, the ache to find meaning and direction diminishing. We can trust Him, believe His words, live knowing that they are true. We don't have to look to a spouse, a career, or anything else to give our life shape and substance. *This* is freedom. *This* is what we crave and long for.

Once we acknowledge and build our lives on a true estimation of God's character and purposes, we can then recognize an essential aspect of our search for meaning: Unless they begin and end with Him, our plans and dreams will fall short. To close this chapter, I'd like to explore why the purposes we establish for our own lives often fail.

It's Really About . . .

Pastor Rick Warren opened his wildly successful book *The Purpose-Driven Life* with these words: "It all starts with God."

> *It's not about you. The purpose of your life is far greater than your own personal fulfillment, your peace of mind, or even your happiness. It's far greater than your family, your career, or even your wildest dreams and ambitions. If you want to know why you were placed on this planet, you must begin with God. You were born by his purpose and for his purpose.*[5]

Perhaps the striking simplicity and honesty of words like these are what have sold millions of Warren's book. Perhaps this simple presentation and forthrightness are what enrage Warren's vitriolic critics. I don't know. But I do know that his words both resonate with and infuriate people. Why? Because we simultaneously want to know and are repelled by the idea that life is not about us. We long to be caught up in something greater and bigger than our finite lives, yet we're terrified that our own happiness and fulfillment may not be the point of the years we're given on earth.

Sadly, mistakenly, many people look to marriage (or a particular person, or raising children) to give them purpose and direction, primarily because they believe that doing so will bring them the greatest personal joy and give them lasting impact on the present or future. But this attempt, beginning with the wrong source and ending with misguided motives, can only fail. If we are to find the purpose we yearn for, it *must* start with God.

We've already looked at why we can trust God with our search for meaning and direction. His goodness and sovereignty assure us that He is able and trustworthy. Yet if we are to experience true freedom with the substance and shape of our lives, we must also admit that life is neither strictly for, nor completely about, us.

"For everything, absolutely everything, above and below, visible and invisible . . . *everything* got started in him and finds its purpose in him" (Colossians 1:16). It couldn't be stated any plainer or more powerfully. *Absolutely everything* begins and finds its objectives in God. That includes me . . . and you . . . and marriage.

People spend their lifetimes trying to find happiness and fulfillment in their own purposes and plans. But as the Bible clearly teaches, "Obsession with self . . . is a dead end; attention to God leads us out into the open, into a spacious, free life" (Romans 8:6). To live the lives we crave, we need to start with God and end with God. Only in *His* purposes can we find the spacious and free life we dream of.

> *It's in Christ that we find out who we are and what we are living for.*
> *Long before we first heard of Christ and got our hopes up, he had his eye*
> *on us, had designs on us for glorious living, part of the overall purpose*
> *he is working out in everything and everyone. (Ephesians 1:11-12)*

We couldn't ask for better than this. Before the world began, the blessed and only Sovereign lovingly trained His eyes on us, designed a *glorious living* for us, part of something larger and grander than anything we could concoct for ourselves. This is the life of purpose we want. And living in it actually brings the deep personal satisfaction that we sometimes expect marriage, a partner, or children to provide.

I urge you, my sisters in Christ, to begin your search for meaning and purpose with God. And please don't skip over this idea just because you have a relationship with the Lord. Many Christians are living aimless and purposeless lives because they haven't authentically wrestled with what they're looking to for direction and meaning, haven't genuinely surrendered to the truth that happiness and purpose come only from God. Certainly, He uses many things to shape us, to bless us, sometimes to break us, but life is ultimately about *His glory*, reflected in those made in His image, echoing mercy and whispering love throughout all eternity.

Don't wait for marriage, for a spouse, for anything to determine "the rest of your life." Start now, asking God to reveal clearly His purposes and plans. His desires for you now, rather than irreconcilably conflicting with the future, will weave together with harmony and grace. And if you are fortunate enough to find the restless ache for purpose and direction quieted before you wed, you will be blessed indeed. Knowing His character and believing He is the source and starting point for all your life will only strengthen your relationships, both now and in the days to come.

If you are already married and have lived for years as if your spouse or your children are the purpose of your life, do not despair. Today, right now, you can turn to God and point the arrow of your life in His direction. It's not too late—it's *never* too late—to live for Him and in Him. I pray that you would, all your remaining days.

Pressing On . . .

1. Question 1 of the Westminster Shorter Catechism, which believers have recited for centuries, asks, "What is the chief end of man?"

What is our purpose? it might have read. The answer: "Man's chief end is to glorify God, and to enjoy him forever."[6] You may have heard or read these words before. If so, try to recall what you thought the first time you encountered these statements. If these words are new to you, spend a couple of minutes considering them. Since the beginning of time, men have tried to discover the meaning of life, and with one question, this catechism seeks to answer all of the queries, end all of the confusion. Do you believe that your purpose is to glorify God and enjoy Him forever? What might this look like in daily life? Which of these two—glorifying or enjoying God—is more difficult for you to understand? Why? Spend some time with the Lord, asking Him to reveal what your life would look like if everything you did honored God and reflected your pleasure in Him.

2. Some people, even some churches, believe that the ultimate purpose of a Christian woman's life is to marry and have children. Have you ever felt or sensed pressure toward this? How are single women treated in your church or your sphere of influence? Have you ever been tempted to consider the single life a "holding pattern" until marriage and children come? Is this idea biblically grounded? If so, or if not, what verses would you use to support your idea?

3. In 2 Timothy 2:21, the apostle Paul revealed, "If you keep yourself pure, you will be a utensil God can use for his purpose. Your life will be clean, and you will be ready for the Master to use you for every good work" (NLT). What are you doing to "keep yourself pure" and "clean"? Are the daily activities in which you engage encouraging or hindering you from being "a utensil God can use for his purpose"? Do you even want to be "ready for the Master to use you"? Spend some time exploring this with the Holy Spirit.

What might you need to cut out or reorganize in order to be used "for every good work"?

4. When faced with difficulties or trials, humans often wonder about God's purposes for their lives. It takes great courage to live by the words of Isaiah 8:17 — "I will wait for the Lord to help us, though he is hiding now. My only hope is in him" (TLB). Interact with the following quote about courage, taken from Nicole Johnson's *Keeping a Princess Heart in a Not-So-Fairy-Tale World*:

> *To be courageous doesn't mean that you are not afraid; it means that fear doesn't win by changing your course. Courage is staying the course in the face of danger. It is sticking with your intended plan of action in the midst of difficulty or uncertainty, without being overcome by fear. . . . Even when we know what to do in the middle of dark uncertainty, we still need courage to do it.*[7]

For which aspects of your life-purpose do you need courage today?

5. The fulfilling and meaningful life we all crave is not only possible but is offered to us in Christ Jesus. But it will not simply *happen*. A series of repetitive days, an overflowing inbox, and the sense that life is not everything we hoped it would be will "just happen," but a purposeful life must be pursued, chased after, often fought for. With God as your starting point and source, brainstorm what practical changes you might want to make in order to grab hold of the kind of significant and satisfying life you desire.

SEVEN

Sex Won't Be an Issue Anymore

IF THERE'S ONE WORD I never imagined would apply to married sex, it's *complicated*. No doubt I'll betray some of my naiveté by confessing this, but I honestly thought sex with my husband would just happen easily, naturally, and, let's not forget, passionately. If someone would have taken me aside before my wedding and described married sex as sometimes complex, sometimes downright problematic, I probably would've assumed she had some sexual hang-up; maybe she needed therapy.

Not that I considered myself an expert on what sex should be like within marriage. But like many of you — single or married — I had my ideas. And none of them would have fallen under the heading "complicated things I need to think through and evaluate my expectations regarding." Yet complicated—beautifully and maddeningly *complicated*—is precisely what sex often becomes.

Even between physically and emotionally healthy spouses who dearly love one another, sex can be (almost simultaneously) frustrating and fabulous. But if you factor in the soul wounds practically every partner received in childhood or as a young adult; if you recognize the enormously varied ways people think and feel about the acts of sex—or about the emotional nakedness that accompanies physically undressing; if you look at sex from nearly any angle, it's easy to see why sexual relations are complex, intricate, and involved.

The complicated network of assumptions and anticipation regarding married sex presents unique concerns for singles and young couples. For some Christians, the longer they wait to get married, the more intense are the expectations they develop for sex. Thinking sex will be the pinnacle experience of their lives, some place a tremendously heavy weight on married intimacy. Others hope that their fears about sex will magically evaporate when they say, "I do." And still others assume that as long as they're able to have sex within marriage, they won't crave anything else; in other words, getting married will keep their sex drive under control. Unfortunately, each of these ideas can lead to serious trouble.

To help us wade through some of the fundamental misconceptions that paralyze or pressurize us, I've invited a dear friend and amazingly gifted communicator to share some of what God has taught her about sexual expectations.

Lorraine Pintus has spent a great deal of the last ten years writing and teaching about holy and healthy sexuality. As the coauthor of three excellent resources on the subject,[1] Lorraine has helped shape my thinking about purity, sexual expression, and how God's Word speaks to these topics. As a mentor, Lorraine has challenged and blessed me, vulnerably sharing her own journey and sagely advising me along the way. As you "listen in" on a recent conversation Lorraine and I had, discussing what she's observed and learned, I have no doubt you'll receive wise counsel and great encouragement from her, as I always do.

Grace . . . Even in Delayed Reactions
A conversation with Lorraine Pintus

Jerusha: *I'd like to start with a big question right off the bat: How common are sexual problems in marriage?*

Lorraine: *As much as it hurts to shatter the dreams people hold on to, I tell the young men and women I speak to that 95 percent of them will experience sexual problems at some point in marriage; the other 5 percent will just be in denial. The truth is, if you have had prior sexual experience, shame and wrong expectations can follow you into the bedroom. If you've had no sexual experience, figuring out another person—a husband or wife—who is wired so differently than you, with unique expectations and needs, can be a* tremendous *challenge. Assumptions arising from our culture, from our spouse, and from our own minds can all create problems in the bedroom, but if couples go into the marriage knowing that these challenges can be normal, they will be much better off. Shattering the lies that everything happens naturally and there will be no struggles really is the best thing I can do for people.*

Jerusha: *Recently, you spoke to a large group of single Christians from around the country. How did they react to these ideas?*

Lorraine: *Many of them tried to understand, but in an audience of any size, there are such vastly different perspectives. It was amazing and heartbreaking for me to witness, once again, how extreme the range of sexual experience in the Christian world has become; it's certainly greater than thirty years ago. It even seems more intense than ten years prior.*

On one extreme, you find young people so sheltered or so naive that all they know about sexual intimacy is what they've seen in movies or read in magazines. *Tragically, most of this media-driven information is based on total fallacies, devoid of relationship; it makes sex seem instantly wonderful—one minute you're a virgin, the next you're a sex goddess. Despite the recent explosion of books exploring Christian sexuality, there's still little patience for the idea that sex may be painful or that it takes time for a couple to learn, to grow, to experiment. The idea that a husband or wife may not immediately be turned-on by exposed skin or even a passionate kiss seems ludicrous to the cinema-fed crowd.*

On the other extreme, you find highly sexualized Christians who have "seen and done it all" (whether because of what has been done to them or because of what they have chosen to do). But here's what most young men and women in this situation do not understand: There is a time delay between the sexual experiences of the past and the mind's ability to process them. I've watched over and over again as women in their thirties struggle to work through the choices or tragedies of their childhood and early adulthood.

Jerusha: *What do you mean?*

Lorraine: *Most often, the consequences of sexual sin are not realized until many years after the experience; we don't immediately feel the full effects of our decisions. I've counseled with many women who had been promiscuous, women who may even have enjoyed sex in the early years of their marriage but then five or six years after the wedding discovered they felt burdened and inhibited, unable to give themselves fully to the joys of their marriage bed. Similarly, the deep regret of abortion doesn't always take hold instantaneously; when a woman becomes pregnant again later in life, going through ultrasounds and feeling a baby move inside her, the agony of past decisions can descend upon her with such force that it threatens her health and her marriage. Women who've been abused sometimes cannot fathom the horror of what happened to them until they want to and/or do have children of their own. Holding a beloved son or daughter in their arms, they wonder how anyone could commit such a heinous act against* *an innocent, helpless child. In some cases, only then does their subconscious mind open the floodgates of past experience; memories that may have been safely dammed up for years become intimately real once again.*

Here's the bottom line, what I'm really getting at: It's so essential that women go into marriage knowing that things will come up. We can all expect and plan for it. Even if you haven't experienced a whole lot sexually, what you thought, what you witnessed as a young child, and what you were told will *play a role in your marriage.*

Jerusha: *How have you seen this unfold in your own marriage?*

She sighs deeply and pauses for a moment.

Lorraine: *Before I get into my own story of how pain and shame revealed themselves in a time delay, let me tell you one thing: I've learned that sex almost defies rational thinking. Try as we might to apply logic and reason to the dynamics of human sexuality (and certainly in many cases it's important that we use these God-given tools), the mystery of sex is far bigger than we can comprehend. We need to lean on a God who's much greater than what we can work out or explain. I don't know that I truly believed that before I began to walk forward in my own healing. Experiencing for yourself that He is able not only to set free but to give* total *freedom—big, expansive, complete, no-tethers-to-it freedom—there's nothing like it.*

The unfolding story of my life has revealed that processing the experiences of my past against the backdrop of who God really is and extending and receiving forgiveness are two of the most important aspects of sexual expression.

Jerusha: *I don't think many people would classify knowing who God is and experiencing forgiveness as significant facets of their sexuality. Tell me how you discovered that. Did that come through your writing and speaking?*

Honest laughter.

Lorraine: *No. At first I really didn't even want to talk or write about sexuality because it was such an area of hurt and failure for me. But God already had me teaching women's retreats, and every time I turned around,* sexual issues confronted me—a wife with no desire for sex after she got married; young women sobbing over the things they'd done, wondering if past sins would exclude them from God's blessing in marriage; hearts splintered and shattered from infidelity or sexual abuse. So much of the hurt in our world could be traced back to sexuality. Sometimes I cried out to God, "There's so much pain out here. Why did You even create sex?" But through years of study and prayer, He's brought me to the place where I can clearly see that He created sex to be perfectly beautiful and intimate. Instead, it's sin, and the father of sin (the Devil), that have twisted and perverted it so heinously. Think about it . . . the Bible uses the picture of a husband and wife to portray the image of Christ and His bride (see Ephesians 5:22-33). Why wouldn't the Enemy go after that image, that oneness? He hates sexual intimacy because, in its purest form, it is to be a picture of Christ and the church. Of course he'd aim to distort this image; that's why we see so much of what we do with sexuality—the ignorance, the denial, the perversion, and the lies. Satan hates holy sex.

Jerusha: *Everything you're saying makes perfect (if tragic) sense. But how do these lies converge with people's expectations?*

Lorraine: *Let me answer that from my own life. My husband was a virgin when we married; I was not. This lie haunted me: "Because of what you did before you got married, you don't deserve to feel pleasure, to have holy, erotic fun with your husband." You see, before I got married, I had an abortion, but it wasn't until eight years into my marriage that I began to face the anguish over my choice. Nowadays, because of ultrasounds, we know that abortion kills a baby inside the womb, but back when I made that decision, such technology was not in widespread use. I believed what the nurse told me: "It's just a blob of tissue. Lots of people do it." I was sure God didn't approve, but was it really that bad?* It's not going to alter my future or anything, *I thought. But years later, as the Holy Spirit revealed the naked reality of my sin, I began to hate myself. I saw that not only had I killed my baby, but I had also wounded my husband by what I'd* *done—I'd robbed him of innocence and freedom. Multiple layers of shame threatened me, and it took traveling to every one of those levels before I could experience genuine healing. Because I've been there, I can tell you that God can walk you through anything. He is able; His grace is real. And God has used my husband, Peter, to flesh out that grace in so many amazing ways.*

Jerusha: *That's incredible. But how exactly has that happened?*

Lorraine: *It started when Peter and I had been dating about three months. I was terrified about what he'd do once he discovered that I wasn't the wonderful Christian girl he thought I was (we'd been leading worship together in our Sunday school class). One night, I couldn't stand it anymore. I had to tell him. He was saving himself for a godly wife. What would he do when he learned that not only was I not a virgin, but six months ago I'd had an abortion? As Peter sat on the couch, I paced the floor in front of him. I was so agitated that I couldn't even look him in the eye. Finally, he pulled me down to sit beside him. Lovingly, but forcefully, Peter said, "Lorraine, tell me what is going on." Haltingly, I admitted my sin. "I'm not who you think I am . . . " I began. Silence followed my confession, but accusations screamed through my mind:* You evil woman! This godly man will want nothing to do with you now that he knows the truth! *I waited for what seemed like an eternity for him to speak, certain that he would tell me it was time for us to break up, time for him to move on.*

A long pause follows. Lorraine remains silent, stuck in the memory of that moment. But I have to know what happened!

Jerusha: *Well, what did he say? Did he tell you that he didn't want to see you anymore?*

Lorraine: *No. Very quietly, but with a certainty that rocked my soul, he asked, "Will . . . you . . . marry . . . me?"*

Jerusha: *Wow; that's grace!*

Lorraine: *Yes, that's grace. And it is a perfect picture of what Jesus does for all of us when it comes to our sexuality. We tell Him the worst we've* done, we expose our filthy rags, and He invites us: "Will you be my spiritual bride?" What I didn't deserve—a second chance, forgiveness, grace—I miraculously received. That's the offer we're all given, and why we can fall so deeply in love with Jesus. But even if I felt freedom and forgiveness that night, certain behaviors and attitudes had attached to my past choices; these took years to undo.

Jerusha: Wow. I think that hits home for everyone. No matter what we've done, aren't there always behaviors and attitudes attached?

Lorraine: You've got it. And if there's something that every young man and woman need to hear before they get married (and potentially every day of their early marriage), it's that getting to the root of their behaviors and attitudes is key. It's not just what happened or didn't happen in our sexual pasts. It's all about the beliefs that become associated with our choices. That's where expectations and assumptions really take hold. I personally battled tying my sin to the act of sex. Sometimes I hated sex. If I'd stayed pure before marriage, I reasoned, I wouldn't have had an abortion. Resentment and blame ensnared my soul in a vicious cycle. I'd try to cover it up, thinking Peter couldn't tell. But my walls were up. I'm so grateful God dealt with me gently, mercifully. Relentlessly, the Lord marched around my walls until, like that miraculous day in Jericho, they tumbled down. I've seen Him rescue countless women, no matter what their story, in this same way. And He's so individual and tender about it! God's is such an intimate love, and I'm continually amazed at how He finds a way (often one that couldn't have worked for anyone else besides that person) to meet needs, to offer forgiveness, to heal the wounds of past abuse or shame.

Jerusha: So I guess sex never stops being an issue?

Full-throttle laughter this time.

Lorraine: It's always an issue, my friend. It just grows and morphs, depending on the phase you're in. Of course, the big picture shouldn't change—we're always called to stay pure and honor God—but the nuances vary endlessly. Sometimes I encounter women who earnestly believe if they stay pure before *marriage, sex will no longer be an issue. After they're married, they won't have to worry about purity anymore. That's a flat-out lie. Purity is a life-long battle, and if people can go into marriage with that expectation, they'll be way ahead of the game.*

My conversation with Lorraine that day continued, but it's time for you and me to break away, to start unpacking some of what we can learn and begin applying it to our own lives. As we press forward, I'd like you to think about a few things: Have you ever authentically evaluated the expectations you have about sex? Can you recognize the attitudes and actions that have attached themselves to the experience (or nonexperience, if you prefer to think of it that way) of your past? How do you feel about what you've read? Are you frustrated that sex might not be as "carefree" as you anticipated? Are you concerned about the choices or wounds of your past "following you into the bedroom"? Do you have a different worry or feeling?

If you're willing to venture with these questions into the complex territory of your heart, I encourage you to put the book down and take whatever time you need to listen, to pray about or journal, to process what the Holy Spirit might bring up. Remember, this book is about allowing God to renovate your thinking. That doesn't happen instantaneously, nor does it happen accidentally.

Deliberately choosing to uncover what you really think and feel about sex (remember, our feelings often point us back to what we actually believe) will open the way for transformation. And as we continually surrender ourselves to the God who answers (see Psalm 116:1), we'll find that "by his mighty power at work within us, [Yahweh] is able to accomplish infinitely more than we would ever dare to ask or hope" (Ephesians 3:20, NLT).

In Context

According to 1 Corinthians 7:1, we're not the only ones with questions about sexuality. The ancient church at Corinth apparently shared our concern about what people should think—and what God thinks—about sex. The apostle Paul opened the seventh chapter of his epistle with the words, "Now about the questions you asked in your letter" (NLT).

From context, it's easy to determine one thing the Corinthians wanted to know: "Is it a good thing to have sexual relations?" (This is how *The Message* translates the latter half of this verse.) Is it okay to have sex at all, they asked, or is it better to stay celibate?

Most of us probably don't wake up with these questions on our mind. Within the church, as well as outside it, sex is widely touted as one of the greatest experiences humans can have. Indeed, most people—the majority of Christians included—imagine their life would be infinitely better if they were having sex regularly, especially with someone they love. Ask a wide sampling of Christian teens what they most look forward to in marriage, and if they're honest, sex will come up nine times out of ten. The simple fact is, whether or not it's "good to have sex" usually doesn't cross the minds of modern people, single or married, Christian or nonbelieving.

But if we are to genuinely evaluate our expectations and assumptions about married sex (or sexuality in general), *this* is the question to start with: Does God like sex, or does He simply allow it? Is it a good thing to have sex?

The passage that follows in 1 Corinthians 7 is an incredibly difficult one, one that biblical scholars have fussed and fretted over for centuries. And I confess that I am neither equipped nor eager to enter the etymological debates bristling around this complicated set of verses. There's one truth from this passage, however, that nearly everyone can agree upon: God created sex and heartily approves of it . . . in context.

Is it a good thing to have sexual relations?

Certainly — but only within a certain context. It's good for a man to have a wife, and for a woman to have a husband. Sexual drives are strong, but marriage is strong enough to contain them and provide for a balanced and fulfilling sexual life in a world of sexual disorder. (verses 1-2)

Our world, like that of the Corinthians, is one of sexual disorder. Every day pain and anguish such as Lorraine described — the abuse and agony that caused her to call out to God, "Why did You even create sex?" — reveal the dysfunctional, distorted way sex drives have consumed and mastered people.

Yet within the strong bonds of marriage we find balance and beauty, fulfillment and freedom. In Song of Songs, with intensity and unashamed passion (enough to make almost anyone red-faced), God communicates the glories of married intimacy. Throughout the Bible, the Divine Author of human sexuality clearly reveals His multifaceted purposes for sex: Comfort and commitment, procreation and pleasure are among His designs for sexual expression in marriage.[2]

Is it a good thing to have sexual relations? According to God, *absolutely*!

And in part, this explains why some people expect and anticipate so much from sex, especially if they have "saved it" for marriage. This also confirms the tragedy of sexual abuse; the fact that God devised sex to be an expression of married intimacy, of unique knowing and precious pleasure, reveals the genuine horror of things like incest and rape.

God *did* intend married sexuality to be incredibly fulfilling. And I wish with all my heart I could end with that wonderful declaration. How I wish I could tell you, "Expect all you want . . . sex with your spouse will be all you dreamed of, and then some!"

There are moments — perhaps even long stretches — when married couples experience glimpses of this. But sadly, because of sin, His original plan, His gloriously perfect blueprint for sexual expression, isn't all we work with on a daily basis.

Roadblocks to Your "Happily Ever After"

Whether or not we recognize it, we battle every day against the intentions of the Evil One, the thief who comes to steal and kill and destroy (see John 10:10). God's enemy is not satisfied simply by making us unhappy and unfulfilled (though he certainly tries to accomplish these sinister goals); the father of lies actually seeks to enslave and annihilate us. The enemy of your soul will do everything he can to steal the joy of sexual purity, kill your desire for what actually brings balance and fulfillment, and destroy God's work in your life.

He tries to make sex about physical pleasure and technique. But God tells us explicitly,

> There's more to sex than mere skin on skin. Sex is as much spiritual mystery as physical fact. As written in Scripture, "The two become one." Since we want to become spiritually one with the Master, we must not pursue the kind of sex that avoids commitment and intimacy, leaving us more lonely than ever — the kind of sex that can never "become one." (1 Corinthians 6:16-17)

Clearly, these verses command those outside of the bonds of marriage to refrain from sexual expression. God reveals it will only leave them "more lonely than ever." But even married couples can engage in "the kind of sex that avoids commitment and intimacy," the kind of sex that leaves people emptier and more wounded than before.

As Gary Thomas so aptly expressed in *Sacred Marriage*, "There are many books that focus on the technical mastery of sex . . . But the true challenge of sex is in its spiritual mastery. A growing, healthy, giving, and selfless sex life is not easy to maintain."[3]

Indeed, added *The Mystery of Marriage* author Mike Mason, "Sex is one of those mysteries which, like prayer, will not yield to technique . . . any approach with a view to technical mastery will be doomed from the start. What the sex life really demands is the loving gift of the self, the sincere devotion of the whole heart."[4]

No wonder sex is so complicated! Satan tricks so many people into looking for the perfect orgasm (if you don't believe me, just pick up the latest edition of *Glamour* or *Cosmo*), when what our souls truly long for is perfect oneness, the loving and selfless gift of intimacy, the sincere devotion of a whole heart.

The Enemy also attempts to twist sex into a selfish pursuit or a manipulative power play. These days, uninhibited by the social constraints that used to keep people from openly discussing sex, men and women talk endlessly and explicitly about their sexual "needs" and "rights," what their partners do or do not "deserve." What's perhaps most disheartening is the way such conversation has wormed its way into the body of Christ.

Fortunately, the Bible speaks directly to these issues. Through the apostle Paul, God expressly commanded, "The marriage bed must be a place of mutuality—the husband seeking to satisfy his wife, the wife seeking to satisfy her husband. Marriage is not a place to 'stand up for your rights.' Marriage is a decision to serve the other, whether in bed or out" (1 Corinthians 7:3-4). How different would our world be if every single Christian went into marriage with this mind-set?

In sexual expression and expectation, as in all things, the Lord urges us to "do nothing from selfishness or empty conceit, but with humility of mind regard one another as more important than yourselves; do not merely look out for your own personal interests, but also for the interests of others" (Philippians 2:3-4, NASB).

If people took just these four verses seriously—if couples determined to serve one another "whether in bed or out," if they did not merely look out for their own interests but humbly placed one another before themselves—there would be a whole lot less divorce, sexual dysfunction, and heartache in the world. But to an entitlement-happy, self-fulfillment-crazy world, the idea that sex is an important way to serve your spouse sounds archaic and bizarre, foolish and fanatical.

The Enemy uses differing levels of desire as well as assumptions about when, where, and how married sex should happen to force couples into opposite corners, ready to fight for their "rights" and get their "needs" met. But the truth is, *different people have different sex drives.*

As I interviewed couples and researched for this book, wives consistently mentioned how surprised they were by the amount of sex their husbands wanted and/or expected. Many of these women, even those married within the last fifteen years when talk about sexuality has been far more candid, told me they never considered that their own sex drive might significantly differ from their husband's.

Before I got married, I honestly believed I would want to have and *actually* would have sex every single day. I thought about sex enough as a single woman to believe that I would be ready whenever Jeramy unbuttoned his shirt. I didn't even bother to factor in my menstrual cycle and how that might affect our intimacy.

I know women who think their husbands should be happy with "whatever they get," maybe a couple of times a week (some added a phrase like "if they're lucky" or "if they're nice"), and still other wives who, whether because of negative experiences from their past or naiveté, staunchly refuse to think about the frequency of their sexual expression. I've also known women who struggle because their husbands want to be intimate far *less* than they do.

Every person thinks and feels about sex uniquely. And because individual physiology plays a huge role in drive and desire, it's often difficult for husbands and wives to understand, let alone live with and respect, one another's sexual longings. That's why it's vitally important that women think about, both before they marry and throughout their marriage, how they might respond during those moments — or seasons — when their sex drive differs from their partner's.

If we don't (or won't), the Enemy will almost certainly take advantage of the situation, pitting spouse against spouse in a battle of needs and wills or escalating sexual tension to such a fever pitch that one or both spouses are tempted to "find help elsewhere." Of course, the Lord would *never* sanction one giving in to that temptation, but we must be aware that withholding intimacy in marriage can make sexual desire all the more difficult to master. This extra pressure benefits no one.

In an effort to avoid altercations of will and need, as well as the torment of increased sexual temptation, consider a couple of details with me, details that may better prepare you to understand your current or future spouse. Let's start with the male sex drive.

According to the best-selling book *Every Man's Battle,* males have a "strong, regular sex drive." Okay, no huge surprise there. That "the human male, because of sperm production and other factors, naturally desires sexual release every forty-eight to seventy-two hours"[5] may not be monumentally shocking either. What often takes women aback is how dramatically this cycle affects a man's ability to withstand sexual temptation, even to concentrate on the daily tasks of his life.

Sadly but truly, some men cruelly manipulate information like this, using it against their wives, demanding that their spouse fulfill sexual needs on schedule with their own "natural" drive for release. Women whose sex drive outstrips their husbands' may similarly utilize their own cyclical drive as a means of control or claim on their husbands.

Such thinking *never* fits with the injunctions of Scripture.

Understood appropriately, however, physiological details like this can help husbands and wives understand why Paul urged couples to continually think of and serve one another, not neglecting their sex life or withholding intimacy.

> *Abstaining from sex is permissible for a period of time if you both agree to it, and if it's for the purposes of prayer and fasting—but only for such times. Then come back together again. Satan has an ingenious way of tempting us when we least expect it. I'm not, understand, commanding these periods of abstinence—only providing my best counsel if you should choose them. (1 Corinthians 7:5-6)*

If you are married, there are *very likely* times you do not want sex but can choose to lovingly serve your partner in that way. There are *very likely* times you are tempted to withhold sex from your partner because of something he did (or did not do). In these moments, when your love and desire are tested, what will you choose? There may not be a biblical imperative for spouses to say yes every time their partner asks for sex, but there *are* clear biblical sanctions against using sex as a means of exercising power or asserting oneself.

Being prepared for and thinking through such things are essential, as is continually acknowledging the role of purity in living a God-honoring life. Whether you're single or married, sexual purity plays a huge part in your life.

This Isn't a "Before and After" Kind of Thing

As Lorraine mentioned, many women view getting married as the end of their journey with purity. I've written about this elsewhere myself,[6] and other esteemed colleagues and mentors of mine have explored this topic at length. In this book, then, I'd like to share with you just a couple of thoughts, specifically related to expectations and assumptions.

Tucked in the thirteenth chapter of the book of Hebrews, we find some immensely important words on the subject: "Let marriage be held in honor by all, and let the marriage bed be kept undefiled" (verse 4, NRSV). It's a verse you may have heard or read several times—and a seemingly straightforward one. But looking at the original language of the New Testament helped me understand the significance of these words a bit better.

In the Greek, the phrase that various translations render "held in honor," "honorable in all," and "give honor to" connotes something of great worth, a precious or costly commodity. The Greek word for what translators call "the marriage bed" is literally *coitus,* a direct reference to the act of sexual intercourse. The injunction that *coitus* "be kept" (elsewhere "guard" or "remain") indicates we should *continually* hold marriage in its proper regard, and the word "undefiled" communicates freedom from any contamination—in other words, *purity.*

With this one, power-packed sentence, the Lord tells us that marriage—and specifically the unique intimacy of sexual connection—is of extraordinary value. So precious are these that both should be consistently and vigilantly kept in untarnished purity. And this statement is directed to each and every one of us, whether single or married.

The forces vying to poison the purity of our minds and actions are manifold. Any of us could rage (almost interminably!) about the difficulties of responsibly navigating the Internet, the movie theater, and personal relationships. Certainly, the easy availability of pornography and the nonchalant way many treat things from flirting to "friends with benefits" to hooking up seem diabolically devised to war against a Hebrews 13:4 lifestyle. And once again, these are not problems strictly outside the church.

Making deliberate and consistent choices about purity may start during the single years, but it *never stops* being an essential part of Christian growth and maturity. Married people, too, need to determine carefully what they will watch, which sites they will visit, what online providers to partner with, and with whom they will interact.

Simply going into marriage understanding that sexual purity is an ongoing journey with the Lord can help couples, but making specific—sometimes difficult—choices will also prove beneficial.

If you know, for instance, that images or chat rooms ensnare you, decide *now* to get help. It may not even be the sexual release you crave; some people find themselves more addicted to the community, to the feelings of love and acceptance they find in computer relationships or from viewing pornographic pictures. Please believe me . . . hope and help are available if you will courageously seek them. As we explored earlier, promiscuity and sexual abuse always affect marriage—as do porn and sexual addiction—but these issues *can be healed*.

Perhaps promiscuity has marked your past, and the idea that precious and undefiled sexual expression can be yours seems impossible. If so, take heart. Our God, the God of second (and infinite!) chances, can walk with you, healing you and reestablishing purity in your heart and mind. Please don't skip over this often-quoted verse: "If we confess our sins to him, he is faithful and just to forgive us and to cleanse us from every wrong" (1 John 1:9, NLT). Will you let the truth of these words pierce you for the sake of healing? The consuming fire of His purity will refine every poor choice, every mistake, *every* wrong; you need only surrender it to Him.

A history of abuse may make you question whether you can ever hold sex in the kind of high regard Hebrews 13:4 commands. Maybe now is the time to ask Him to reveal Himself as the God of hope and comfort in *your* life, over your past experiences. Do you know Him as the God who redeems lost years and broken trust? I personally cherish the words of Joel 2:25-26, which proclaim,

I will make up to you for the years
That the swarming locust has eaten,
The creeping locust, the stripping locust and the gnawing
*   locust . . .*
You will have plenty to eat and be satisfied
And praise the name of the LORD your God,
Who has dealt wondrously with you;
Then My people will never be put to shame. (NASB)

The shame of your past does *not* have to determine the hope of your future. He can and will redeem the years the "locusts" ate, whether the swarming infestation came through the sins of another person inflicted on you or the choices of your own wayward heart. You can be satisfied and praise the name of the God who deals mercifully with you. In Him, there is life and life abundant (see John 10:10).

Wherever you've been, whatever you've chosen, whatever's been done to you, you can choose now to "honor marriage, and guard the sacredness of sexual intimacy between wife and husband" (Hebrews 13:4). Deciding to live with this mind-set, now and for the rest of your life, will help keep your expectations about purity in line with God's.

But once again, we've tackled a huge subject and raised a good deal more questions than we could possibly answer in one chapter. Sex is so incredibly *complicated*! Perhaps that's why Paul wrote these words to his friends at Corinth: "Sometimes I wish everyone were single like me—a simpler life in many ways! But celibacy is not for everyone any more than marriage is. God gives the gift of the single life to some, the gift of the married life to others" (1 Corinthians 7:7).

Whether you are single or married, your life is a gift. Your sexuality, too, is a gift. If you've struggled with sex, if you've been wounded in the past or are being wounded presently, I know it must be very difficult to accept those words. But I pray that the truth of Scripture, coupled with whatever means God would use to heal your heart, will convince you that God has specifically gifted you with *your* life, with *your* drives and desires. I also pray—now that we've opened the door to these important ideas—that you will press on, journeying with the Lord to explore the specific areas in which you have expectations or assumptions, needs and challenges.

Pressing On . . .

1. How do movies and television generally portray sexual relations? After reading this chapter, do you think this perspective helps or hurts married couples in the long run? What are two practical ways you can guard against the onslaught of sexual images and ideas constantly bombarding you through the media?

2. Read 1 Thessalonians 4:3-4: "God wants you to be holy, so you should keep clear of all sexual sin. Then each of you will control your body and live in holiness and honor" (NLT). How does this verse strike you? Do you want to be holy? What about honorable? Does that sound as exciting and desirable to you as being sexy or alluring? Why or why not? Spend some time exploring this with the Holy Spirit. Ask Him to reveal the true nature of holiness and honor to you. Read this command with regard to holiness: "Let yourselves be pulled into a way of life shaped by God's life, a life energetic and blazing with holiness" (1 Peter 1:15). How does that sound?

3. This chapter talked at length about the complicated nature of married sexuality. Consider Paul's words in 1 Corinthians 7:7: "Sometimes I wish everyone were single like me—a simpler life in many ways!" Discuss or journal about the reasons Paul might have said

this. If you are married, how can you use the complex nature of your sexual relationship to glorify God and serve your partner? If you are single, how might you adjust your thinking about sex so as to prepare for marriage?

4. I love the words of Psalm 103:10-11: "He has not punished us for all our sins, nor does he deal with us as we deserve. For his unfailing love toward those who fear him is as great as the height of the heavens above the earth" (NLT). Whether or not you've sinned sexually, these are amazing words of hope and forgiveness. No matter where you've been or what you've done, His mercy can cover you. Use these verses as a prayer of praise and petition, depending on your need and desire. Honestly explore with the Lord your history with sex and receive His forgiveness where needed.

5. *Note: Though most of the questions in these Pressing On sections are appropriate for small-group discussion, the following may best be explored on your own or between you and one other person, perhaps a trusted accountability partner.*

Throughout this chapter, we talked about attitudes and actions that attach themselves to sexual struggles. Now that you've looked at your past with the Spirit, take some time to authentically investigate the thoughts and behaviors that have affixed themselves to your own battles. For instance, if masturbation or pornography has been an issue for you, what beliefs have you associated with this activity? If sexual acts with a boyfriend or another woman have been a problem for you, what thoughts and attitudes have been connected to your decisions? Remember, our goal, and Christ's desire for us, is a transformed mind, so be honest!

To help, I'll leave you with a word about His awesome power. May this prayer remind you of His ability to change you, *no matter what your situation*: "Ah Lord GOD! . . . You have made the heavens and the earth by Your great power and by Your outstretched arm! Nothing is too difficult for You" (Jeremiah 32:17, NASB).

EIGHT

I'll Feel Pretty
(and Witty and Bright)[1]

PRIOR TO MEETING AND marrying Jeramy, I went through a five-year battle with the mirror, distrusting and disliking what it reflected to me. Despite the fact that I regularly received compliments on my appearance, enjoyed the attention of men interested in dating me, and seemed relatively confident, the twenty-year-old me hated the shape of my body. I detested the easy-to-break-out skin on my face.

Truthfully, I had a conflicted relationship with more than my physical appearance; I couldn't understand why God gave me a body in the first place . . . it was such a hassle, with all its messy needs and uncontrollable urges. I didn't—or couldn't—wrap my mind around verses like these: "Since the Master honors you with a body, honor him with your body! . . . Remember that your bodies are created with the same dignity as the Master's body" (1 Corinthians 6:13,15).

My body . . . an honor? My body . . . created with the same dignity as the Master's? It seemed impossible to believe. Some days, I felt that I *should* and *ought to* believe it, but probably never would.

This book isn't the place to chronicle my struggle with disordered eating, excessive exercise, and obsessive concern about my appearance.[2] But those things were certainly part of my experience prior to marriage. And the vicious tentacles of their terror, which wrapped around the deep recesses of my heart and mind, continued to squeeze life out of me even after I fell in love with Jeramy.

Naively, I thought that once I *knew* someone loved me (demonstrated by a ring on my left hand's fourth finger), I would never worry about my appearance again. Well, maybe I wasn't quite that idealistic. Perhaps I just believed that love, and eventually marriage, would so mitigate my struggle with feeling attractive or desirable that it wouldn't be that important anymore.

Countless single women before and after me have believed similarly, convinced that their struggles with insecurity—inextricably connected to their body image and appearance—would disappear (or at least dramatically lessen) with marriage. The general reasoning seems to be, "When I get married, I'll know that someone [my spouse] thinks I'm attractive, so I'll finally [and always] *feel* pretty."

Sadly, for me and many other women, this simply doesn't pan out. For women who remain single year after year, the intimate yet tragic tie between self-worth and body image can become ever stronger. For married women, fears about "letting themselves go" or "not pleasing" their spouse can plague the mind and heart, sending them frantically looking for the next "sure-fire diet," the next "proven results" workout.

Before Jeramy and I met, God had already helped me make huge strides in recovering from my body-image issues. I had recently gotten my period back, and though this may not sound like a cause for celebration to you, the return of my "womanhood" and the rediscovered hope of having children one day gave me a new lease on life.

Pretty early in our relationship, Jeramy and I talked about my past struggles and current state (I still considered myself in recovery). He seemed genuinely concerned for me and unfazed by the things I confessed. *This is exactly what I hoped for!* I thought. *An understanding man who wants to see—maybe even help—me embrace and enjoy rather than despise my body.* He seemed to find me attractive, and I almost believed that I could be.

Almost . . . but not quite. When Jeramy proposed a few months later, my ecstasy could hardly have been greater. I felt free and full and, for the first time, at peace about my body. But as with all emotional highs, this extreme joy diminished with time. The reality of being engaged descended heavy and hard. Don't get me wrong: Engagement can be a beautiful period, a wonderful time to prepare for your wedding and life beyond. It can also, however, be a rather difficult and maddening season. Unfortunately, Jeramy and I experienced much more of the latter than the former.

Our fiery personalities and intense stubbornness were exposed in premarital counseling. One godly mentor actually asked us to prayerfully consider how sure we were about going through with the wedding. The unhealthy patterns that I'd been establishing for years were agonizingly difficult to break, and, when things were hard, I was *not* an easy person to be with. The understanding and sensitivity Jeramy showed me the night we first talked about my struggles with body image and related issues . . . well, let's just say it wasn't always there. He couldn't understand some of my entrenched behaviors or irrational fears. I thought he would help me continue to recover, but I often found that I didn't really want his almost physician- or father-like care.

I didn't feel so pretty around him anymore. I felt messy and exposed and not good enough. But dreams die hard, and I tenaciously clung to the assumption that marriage would make it all get better, or go away entirely.

We saw a couple of different counselors during our premarital work, including the woman who had walked with me through the most intense portion of my recovery a few years previously. Dr. Harvey was a genuine blessing to us during this time, helping Jeramy see where I had come from and the path on which I was determinedly committed to walk.

Then came our wedding day—full of promise and passion. Ours was a fairy-tale ceremony and reception, evidenced by pictures showing Jeramy and me leaving the church in a cascade of bubbles. We honeymooned on the unique and nontouristy island of Tortola, a paradise hidden in the British Virgin Islands. Perhaps it was there that the bubbles started to burst.

I was afraid to eat too much on our honeymoon, convinced that not working out for a week would lead to weight gain. Whereas I previously thought being naked and unashamed before my husband would be natural and easy, I wondered instead if he saw the imperfections in my figure with disdain or disgust. I wanted to be free, to give myself to Jeramy fully, but I felt hindered and inhibited by my self-focus, my perpetual concern with how he saw me and what I looked like.

I'm not proud to admit these things to you. In many ways, these are painful memories to revisit. I wanted to be the confident wife, assured of his affection and buoyed up by his loving gaze. But even as Jeramy gave these things to me—he seemed to delight in my body in every way—I couldn't trust them. I felt desperate and confused. In his arms, through his kisses, wasn't I supposed to feel like the most beautiful woman in the world? Was marriage *not* going to give me security in my appearance, as I envisioned it would?

When I realized it wouldn't—when it became clear to me that no matter how much he loved me, Jeramy couldn't make me feel perpetually pretty—it was extremely difficult for me not to return to the "safe" patterns of rigid control over body and food that I had developed in my teenage years. Sheerly by God's grace, I successfully battled many of the urges (while falling prey to others) and continued to heal.

Through ten years of marriage, I've come to see that Jeramy's love and his enjoyment of my body are great gifts to me. They remind me what is true when I doubt. They strengthen and encourage me when I'm weak. These gifts do not *define* my feelings about my body or appearance, but they do nourish and uplift me.

If you're anything like me, though, the statements in that last paragraph beg an obvious question: Then what *does* define the thoughts and feelings about my physicality?

In the limited space I have here, it would be impossible to describe the journey of these last fifteen years—the ten of my marriage and the five before it, when I battled so fiercely with body-image issues. Because of my personal struggles, a good portion of my devotional life has been focused on figuring out what God's perspective on my body is. I would love to communicate all that He's taught me, but this is a book about marital expectations, not body image.

Assumptions about marriage and physical appearance do intersect, however, which is why I'd like to share with you these truths I cling to: It *is* an honor to have a body, and I have a choice as to whom (or what) I will honor with my physical presence. I can honor the Master, in whose glorious image I am created, with whose dignity my body and soul are forever stamped. Or I can honor the world, the lust of the eyes and the pride of life. If I choose the latter, destruction and obsession are natural consequences. But as I've seen time and time again, when I decide to live in the former—in His Truth and Grace—I can enjoy this body He's given me. I *can* honor Him with it.

The verses I quoted earlier, from 1 Corinthians, actually mean what they say: It *is* an honor to have this body God's given me. And the whole counsel of God is masterfully interwoven with proven and lasting wisdom about how to deal with the bodies we have. The Bible has revealed itself as wise in the practical living out of my days. This shouldn't have surprised me; after all, it *is* the inerrant Word of God. But really knowing this, letting it penetrate the darkest and most unconvinced parts of my mind, and actually *living it out* on a daily basis have been an incredible ride for me.

You may never have struggled, as I did, with eating issues or a neurotic obsession about your appearance. But I wonder if you've ever thought that marriage would settle the questions of your desirability and attractiveness. I wonder if you've ever dreamed about feeling pretty because someone was there, someone who'd tell you, "You are beautiful," someone who'd make you feel safe or full or longed for.

If you've ever had a thought like this, I invite you to walk with me through the next few pages, investigating what—and more importantly *Who*—can actually satisfy our desire to be preferred, to be adored, to be alluring and delightful. By focusing on God's truth, singles can squarely face concerns about appearance and body image *before* marriage, thus alleviating potentially damaging expectations. And for those of us who are already married, we can embrace the freedom and life that come with living the truth about our physical bodies, rather than an illusion.

Why We Want To . . .

Why do women want to feel beautiful?

A fascinating question, isn't it? If you ask some, the answer is simple: We've been conditioned by society, and years of oppression, to believe that beauty is what really matters. The culture around us teaches that women who are attractive have more to offer: They are the powerful and strong and "together" ones; these are the women who "get" men; they succeed and relish life.

Most assuredly, our society—along with a myriad of cultural mores—has communicated these messages. The world we live in urges us to focus on image, on appearance, on how our physical presence affects the people around us. A woman who can get men to turn their heads as she walks by is esteemed by our beauty-mad culture.

But is there nothing more? Is this all that's behind my own, and so many other women's, desire to be beautiful, to be delightful to the eyes and mind of someone we love? Gratefully, no. There *is* something more.

Beneath the piles of societal rubbish, obscured from view by the cultural milieus that hold us in bondage, we discover that God speaks about beauty as well as why we long for it. And what He has to say may shock you.

What if part of the reason we long to be beautiful is because God Himself is beautiful? What if we want to reveal and enjoy beauty because God Himself does? What if women were intimately and lovingly designed to participate in God's beauty by revealing it on the earth? Well, He *is* . . . He *does* . . . and we *were*. *You* were created to reflect His beauty, and that is part of why you want to feel attractive.

Certainly, the forces arrayed around and against us would like to pervert this pure and holy desire. Society, and the enemy of souls, would like you to focus on your own beauty rather than *His,* which you were created to reflect. The slings and arrows of the Evil One, aimed so carefully at society and culture, lodge in the hearts and minds of people everywhere, convincing them that they must pursue and create beauty rather than participate and enjoy that which has been created for and in us by God. And most treacherously, the twisted and toxic lie that beauty means only one thing and looks only one way worms its way into the thoughts of many.

But these perversions of truth should not—*must* not—distract us from Truth Himself. The Word of God continually describes God as beautiful, glorious, splendorous. With and by the psalmist, we are urged to seek and delight in His beauty: "One thing I have asked from the LORD, that I shall seek: That I may dwell in the house of the LORD all the days of my life, to behold the beauty of the LORD and to meditate in His temple" (Psalm 27:4, NASB).

So many of us have sung the gorgeous praise choruses inspired by these verses from Psalm 27, but how many of us have actually stopped to think about the "beauty of the LORD"? Is it physical . . . is it tangible . . . is it *real*?

We know from Scripture that God does not have a human body. But the Word also reveals that everything about God is beautiful. He is arrayed in majesty: "O my soul, bless GOD! GOD, my God, how great you are! beautifully, gloriously robed" (Psalm 104:1). His name is glory itself: "Shout 'Hallelujah!' because GOD's so good, sing anthems to his beautiful name" (Psalm 135:3). And His thoughts are perfect expressions of the splendor that is His: "Your thoughts—how rare, how beautiful! God, I'll never comprehend them!" (Psalm 139:17).

The Bible also reveals that the Lord's beauty is manifested in tangible ways: "GOD made the heavens—royal splendor radiates from him, a powerful beauty sets him apart" (Psalm 96:5-6). His glory is reflected on the earth in physical presences: through a sunset crashing meteor-like into the Pacific Ocean, through the quiet serenity of a hidden mountain lake, through the mist enshrouding Mount Everest's summit. Truly, "the heavens tell of the glory of God. The skies display his marvelous craftsmanship" (Psalm 19:1, NLT). What do you think the words *glory* and *marvelous* mean here? They hint at nothing less than the most magnificent and ravishing beauty!

And what of this word *craftsmanship*? A similar term—translated by many biblical scholars as *workmanship*—appears in Ephesians 2:10. But in Ephesians, humans are the *workmanship* described: "For we are His workmanship, created in Christ Jesus for good works, which God prepared beforehand so that we would walk in them" (NASB).

Now, I love this verse, but I always struggled with that word *workmanship*. It brought to my mind some kind of primitive art. In the Greek, however, this word is *poeima,* from which we get our English word *poem*. And poetry is no crude art form; rather, it takes tremendous skill and precision to craft a poem well. And what we translate *workmanship*, what I mistakenly thought of as a rough and unsophisticated artistic expression, actually means nothing less than an incomparable work of genius. This means that as His *poeima*, you are a glorious masterpiece.[3]

Nowhere is God's beauty more evident than through the crown of His creation, the human. Designed—as nothing else on this earth—to reflect His image, we were made to participate in His beauty. He wants us to reveal the unique and amazing way we have been patterned in the likeness of Beauty Himself. He longs for you to display, in a way that *no one else can,* His glorious image. To think . . . you are an integral part of the pinnacle of His work—it's stunning, isn't it?

And incredibly difficult to believe. Tragically, because women (and men) have been deceived into believing that beauty means only one thing and looks only one way, the innate desire within us to enjoy and reflect beauty becomes twisted into a reckless and endless pursuit of a *certain type* of physical beauty. And so women utilize everything from the relatively innocuous wearing of makeup to the dangerous plastic surgeries they hope will give them a particular shape or form (defined by the world as "beautiful") to make themselves feel pretty or attractive.

C. S. Lewis brilliantly described this in *The Screwtape Letters,* a remarkable book that uses correspondence between an "older" demon and his young apprentice to describe how the Enemy works in the world. In the following selection, Lewis illumined what happens when humans believe beauty looks only one way:

*It is the business of . . . great masters [Screwtape is referring to the
powers of evil] to produce in every age a general misdirection of what
may be called sexual "taste." This they do by working through the
small circle of popular artists, dressmakers, actresses and advertisers
who determine the fashionable type. The aim is to guide each sex
away from those members of the other with whom spiritually helpful, happy, and fertile marriages are most likely. . . . And that is not
all. We have engineered a great increase in the license which society
allows to the representation of the apparent nude (not the real nude)
in art, and its exhibition on the stage or the bathing beach. It is all
a fake, of course; the figures in the popular art are falsely drawn;
the real women in bathing suits . . . are actually pinched in and
propped up to make them appear firmer and more slender . . . than
nature allows a full-grown woman to be. . . . As a result we are
more and more directing the desires of men to something which does
not exist — making the role of the eye in sexuality more and more
important and at the same time making its demands more and more
impossible. What follows you can easily forecast!*[4]

We can easily forecast what happens because we see it every day:
women starving themselves for attention and approval, undergoing
radical procedures to form themselves in the likeness of celebrities,
or simply complaining—with venom—that they are not what they
"should be." What is most tragic, perhaps, is that these women are chasing an illusion, an impossibility, something that—quite simply—*does
not exist.*

No human attempt at mastering beauty will ever satisfy the true
craving of our hearts, which is to reveal and reflect *His* beauty. If we
seek to show off His splendor, we will discover that every human, no
matter how plain or homely according to the world's standards, can
gloriously unveil His beauty.

We desperately need fresh perspective on beauty. And I love the way Bible scholar Eugene Peterson directs us back to ancient wisdom in his rendering of the following well-known verses about beauty from 1 Timothy 2:9-10: "I want women to get in there with the men in humility before God, not primping before a mirror or chasing the latest fashions but doing something beautiful for God and becoming beautiful doing it."

Embracing the beauty God has placed in each one of us does not equal more time spent in front of the mirror, on the elliptical machine, or at the day spa. It means taking part in His glorious plan for the world and *becoming beautiful doing it.*

As is always true, when we seek first the kingdom and His righteousness (see Matthew 6:33), we find what we are looking for. It may not take the same form nor have the same shape as we imagined, but what we really crave and ache for is *always* fulfilled in Christ.

You were created by Beauty Himself. You were created for glory and splendor, as a reflection of the Perfect Majesty who designed you. You have been invited to take part in His magnificence through the ongoing work of revelation and creation. The question is, will you believe it? Will you actually choose to live this out?

Very few do. The world lives in the grip of the Enemy, who skillfully and ferociously deceives people into pursuing "little *b*" beauty rather than "capital *B*" Beauty. And tragically, most of us Christians live somewhere in the middle, straddling the fence between worldly allurements and the hope that what He says might be true.

There is nothing wrong with wanting to feel attractive or desirable. I believe these longings were designed by God to draw us to Himself, the Author and Perfecter of everything beautiful. But I also know that our pure desires have been infected by the poisonous lies of the world. We cannot wholeheartedly trust our own longing to be beautiful or pleasing to someone because it is so tainted with sin. Still, we cannot throw the proverbial baby out with the bathwater. We cannot deny that we want to feel lovely, be desired, and reveal splendor. Too many Christians and too many churches have tried this approach, twisting Scriptures and claiming that God wants nothing to do with physical beauty. This neither honors God nor quiets the restless ache within our souls. We *need* beauty; we need to understand and embrace it. It is part of who we are and who we are to become.

Now that we know a little bit about why we long for beauty, let's look at how this desire plays out in relationships. Because so many people believe that marriage will give them peace and confidence in their physical presence, we need to understand how relationships and beauty intersect.

Power or Purity . . . You Make the Call

Our physical bodies, beautifully reflective of God's glory and splendor, can be used in many ways. We can give and receive pleasure through the touch of a hand, a warm embrace, or a simple smile. We can communicate joy or sorrow with our facial expressions. There is an infinite number of ways our bodies can be used.

In relationships with others, we're often confronted with the question, "Will we use our physical presence as a weapon of power or an instrument of purity?" And this question is nowhere more relevant and profound than in the realm of romance.

Here on earth, we are so sorely—and continually—tempted to use our bodies as means to an end: a tool for getting what we want, manipulating others, or making ourselves feel safe and secure. Whether we do this by trying to attract others or by trying to repel them (thereby "proving" that we are not worthy of love or intimacy), we are quite adept at wielding our bodies as weapons.

Singles face a unique battle in this arena since the physical release of sex is reserved by God only for marriage. The world tells us we should use our sexuality—whether or not we have intercourse with another person—to get what we want: love, affection, attention, even orgasm. If you believe what the media tells you, you might think being sexy or alluring is nonnegotiable, that sex is the pinnacle experience of humanity.

Though married men and women have God's blessing to enjoy sex with their spouse, they are *definitely* not immune to the struggle between purity and perversion. Even in a loving and committed relationship, people are tempted to use their bodies as weapons of power, either manipulating or withholding sex from one another. Tragically, misguided husbands and wives often look outside of marriage for the approval and validation sometimes not found within it.

A sad but frequent attachment to the myth "When I get married, I'll always feel pretty" is the thought "When I get married, I'll know that someone thinks I'm attractive, so no one else's opinion will matter." Wives often find, however, that they don't feel perfectly desired or approved of by their husbands. They may be tempted by fantasy or adultery, believing that someone else's opinion actually *does matter*, and matters quite a bit more than their spouse's. Even a woman who doesn't feel disillusioned in her marriage may be surprised by the realization that she still wants other men to find her attractive and alluring.

This happened to a dear friend of mine, Bridgette. Nothing was particularly "wrong" in her relationship with Jeff, a devoted husband and a godly man. Actually, they had a pretty great marriage, by all accounts. Bridgette never imagined that her work with a short-term mission project would put her in a position of having to decide whether she'd use her body as a weapon of power or an instrument of purity.

But as Bridgette worked more and more closely with a single man on the mission team, she noticed he seemed to find her attractive. She could just sense it. And it disturbed her even more to acknowledge that she *wanted* him to find her desirable and lovely. Bridgette told me, "He treated me like I was the only woman in the world and the greatest, too. I found myself wanting to hang out with him because I liked that feeling."

Admittedly, it was a confusing time for my friend. Some hard questions started to surface in Bridgette's mind: *Do I really love Jeff?* and *Am I capable of being completely committed to the same person for my whole life? How can I be attracted to other people,* she wondered, *if I'm supposed to love only Jeff?*

Bridgette has some great advice for both single and married women:

Never say never. I always used to think, How could people have affairs? *or even,* How could she be flirting with that guy? She's married! *I've discovered that if I'm not careful, that could be me. Only by God's grace and in staying close to Him can I live out my vows to love and be faithful to Jeff.*

I've also come to see that it's unrealistic to think the only attractive person in the world is my husband. Knowing that I (and you!) will be attracted to other people—and it doesn't mean we love our husbands any less—can be a tremendous relief because we don't have to act on that attraction.

People talk these days about "being true to their hearts" and going with an affair, but that is not being true. Many of us are vulnerable to those men who will give us attention and communicate the things we want to hear—whether verbally or with their eyes: "You are worth pursuing; you are beautiful; you are desirable and special." It's flattering to be noticed and sought out, rather than invisible and "used" (often the case for wives and mothers). And these feelings come over us so subtly and so slowly.

We really have to be careful, to stay close to God and know what He says about us. I guess I thought that when Jeff became my husband, God would take away my desires to have affection from anyone but him.

When that didn't happen, I was afraid to talk to other women about being attracted to anyone else.

Finally, I mentioned it in an offhand way to my friend who's a stay-at-home mom. I work and was saying that she was so lucky not to have to deal with men in the workplace. She said, "Bridgette, you can be attracted to the guy who comes to install your hardwood floor." Hearing that from her made me realize that most women (I'm tempted to say every woman) will be attracted to someone else in the course of marriage.

The difference, it seems to me, is that people who end up in affairs let the little steps progress. They linger on a glance or dream about a comment; they stop going back to God for their approval and validation. I don't want that to be me. And that's why when and if I feel attracted to someone else, I choose Jeff, I choose life, I choose God.

Regardless of our stage of life, we are continually confronted with the choice between pursuing power and purity. The sad fact is, many choose power, only to discover the control or influence they thought would be theirs slips from their grasp. Only as we choose to use our bodies and our beauty as instruments of purity do we discover life, peace, hope, and love—in short, everything we crave.

And though this is what we really long for—on the deepest and most intimate level—we are also terrified of being rejected, forgotten, invisible, or unnoticed.[5] Most of us will do virtually anything to ward off these feelings. But this is not the path of Life. Instead, God commands us:

> Do not let sin control the way you live; do not give in to its lustful desires. Do not let any part of your body become a tool of wickedness, to be used for sinning. Instead, give yourselves completely to God since you have been given new life. And use your whole body as a tool to do what is right for the glory of God. (Romans 6:12-13, NLT)

"Use your whole body" . . . that's quite a challenge, isn't it? Thankfully, God puts His grace behind every directive, His power behind every promise. We can live Romans 6 lives because we know and love the Romans 6 God. We can reject the temptation to become tools of wickedness because we have a Savior who enables us to "do what is right for the glory of God."

This time in your life—whether you are single or married—is a time to learn how to use your body as an instrument of purity, of righteousness, of love. If you've been manipulating others with your body or beauty, now is the time to stop. If you're on the flip side, if you've tried to bury your God-given glory or have doubted for so long that you have any beauty to reveal, now is the time to be healed. There is great hope in God, who promises to transform us.

I don't know what the journey of your sanctification will look like or what it will include. Perhaps you need professional therapy to deal with the wounds of your past or the struggles you currently face. If so, don't be afraid. Only "fools are headstrong and do what they like; wise people take advice" (Proverbs 12:15). You will show and gain genuine wisdom if you listen to godly counsel. I've been blessed to see three different counselors, one during my eating-disordered days and two after my postpartum depressions (but that's a story for another book).

Perhaps you need to stop trying to garner the favor of others and start looking to God for your approval and worth. Perhaps you need to believe in and *live out* the truth that you are an incomparable masterpiece, created by God to reveal and participate in beauty. Whatever your journey may entail, I know that God will walk with you, guiding and directing you in personal and powerful ways.

Marriage will not make you feel perpetually pretty. It won't make you feel perfectly desirable or attractive. But it can help you reveal beauty in new and wonderful ways. If you marry or are married, be ready for another unfolding of God's plan, a new level of learning how to live in and reflect His beauty.

Pressing On . . .

1. In his book *The Christian in Complete Armour*, seventeenth-century pastor William Gurnall wisely observed, "It is [the] image of God reflected in you that so enrages hell; it is this at which the demons hurl their mightiest weapons."[6] Beauty is a battleground on which countless victims have fallen prey to the slings and arrows of our enemy. As we affirm the beauty that God places within every one of us, we war against the lies of hell that strip individuals of their dignity and worth. But what happens when we battle the forces around us? How can we prepare ourselves for this fight? Read 2 Corinthians 10:3-5 and Ephesians 6:10-18. Let's not be ignorant of the reality of spiritual warfare. Instead, let us embrace the weapons God has given us and be used by Him to wage war on hell's most pernicious lies.

2. As we begin to see the physical effects of aging on our body and beauty, toxic thoughts may surface (or *re*surface) . . . with a vengeance! Authors Evelyn and James Whitehead noted, "When the body is love's only abode, change becomes an enemy."[7] How do you feel about getting older? How does this quote affect you? Would it be possible to think of change not as an enemy but as something else? A gift? A challenge? An invitation? Which of these metaphors (or one of your own) suits you best? How might thinking of aging in this way transform your experience of it?

3. What did you make of these verses: "I want women to get in there with the men in humility before God, not primping before a mirror

or chasing the latest fashions but doing something beautiful for God and becoming beautiful doing it" (1 Timothy 2:9-10)? Did you know that in most written fairy tales, there are no physical descriptions of the characters to detract from the beauty of their virtue? Have you ever seen someone "beautify" before your eyes as they do something beautiful for God? How might you begin to apply these verses, and the truths within them, to your daily life?

4. Read 1 Peter 3:3-5:

> *Don't be concerned about the outward beauty that depends on fancy hairstyles, expensive jewelry, or beautiful clothes. You should be known for the beauty that comes from within, the unfading beauty of a gentle and quiet spirit, which is so precious to God. That is the way the holy women of old made themselves beautiful. (NLT)*

Notice that Peter did not condemn beauty. Instead, he told us how to attain it. The "holy women of old *made themselves beautiful*" by focusing on the *right kind* of beauty. As we develop inner beauty, the physical reflection of God's splendor becomes more attractive to all around us. How are you currently developing the kind of beauty Peter described? What would you *like* to be doing to develop the beauty of a "gentle and quiet spirit"?[8]

5. When I was a child, I loved Margery Williams' book *The Velveteen Rabbit*. I recently read this story to my six-year-old daughter, and a phrase practically jumped off the page and bit me: "Once you are real you can never be ugly again, except to people who don't understand."[9] When we are living our true identity—as masterpieces created to reveal splendor—we can never be ugly, except to

those who don't understand. How easy or difficult is it for you to embrace your heritage as a daughter of Beauty, as one who reflects glory and majesty? How do you think denying your beauty makes your Creator feel? How would you like to view your body and your physical presence? What steps might you take to make this vision a reality?

NINE

I'll Have a Happy Family

MOST PEOPLE APPROACH MARRIAGE with certain expectations about how a family should, and will, function. Yet when marriage causes relationships with extended family members to change, when parents or spouses disappoint us, when the "new family" a couple begins to build differs from the families in which they grew up, and when adding children to the mix affects these things (along with everything else!), husbands and wives can quickly become disillusioned.

The desire to be part of a big happy family in which everyone gets along with everyone else is a good one, I believe. Remember, God created us for the ultimate "happily ever after" (heaven). But here on earth there are no perfect marriages . . . or perfect families. Building a family—and blending two extended families—is one of the most amazing and heart-wrenching challenges of life.

Melody, a dear friend of mine, went through a lonely and difficult valley when, only a few years after her wedding, the dream of having "one big happy family" shattered. Nobody in her family committed any massive sins; none of them even disliked each other. But through a series of little hurts and minor disappointments, Melody allowed a wall of bitterness to slowly form around her heart.

I pray Melody's story will encourage you to evaluate what might happen to your family dynamics if and when you get married. If you're already building a marriage and family, I hope that Melody's words will challenge you to identify any assumptions you've held on to, taking them to the only One who can heal and reorder them.

Equipped to Love . . . and Forgive
As told by Melody Drake

My husband and I met at a barbecue on my college campus. Though Garret had graduated a few years earlier, he came to this particular gathering at the urging of his younger brother. I had seen Garret at church over summer break and had often tried to meet him. All such attempts—much to my disappointment—had been unsuccessful.

When I noticed him at the barbecue, I seized the opportunity, went right up to him, and introduced myself. We launched into a great conversation, but a short while later, after looking at his watch, Garret informed me that he had to get home to have dinner with his mother. He currently lived in my hometown, six hours from where I attended college, and had planned to spend time with his mom, who lived near my school, before he traveled back. Garret's commitment to her and the date they had made impressed me—a lot. He invited me to come along, and I jumped at the chance.

From that point on, we were a couple. Because of where we both lived, however, with six hours separating us, our dating experience was largely long-distance. Nonetheless, this didn't stop us from getting very close, very fast.

As our relationship became more serious, I began to cultivate a friendship with his parents (remember, they lived in the town where I attended college). I often ended up at their house on Wednesday nights—sometimes I would stop by to borrow videos; other times we would have dinner, and our evenings would usually end with a phone call from Garret. I enjoyed my Wednesday forays to his parents' house: I got to know them; I heard stories about Garret; and I enjoyed the relationship we were building.

Seven months after our first date, Garret asked me to marry him. Four months after that, we said, "I do." Our long-distance, whirlwind romance became a marriage less than a year after we met.

The thrill of building a life together, mixed with the shock of actually living with a spouse, marked our first years of marriage. One thing, however, remained constant: We both enjoyed each other's parents.

I had always dreamed of getting married and bringing two families together to make one big happy family. What I didn't count on was the fact that people are not raised in exactly the same ways. All parents do not parent the same, and values often differ. Though our folks seemed to enjoy each other well enough when they met on various occasions, my parents and in-laws didn't strike up the friendship I had hoped they would.

After four years of marriage, I became pregnant with our first child. My folks openly expressed their joy and excitement upon hearing the news that their tenth grandchild was on his way. Garret's parents, however, did not react with the same enthusiasm. Though they claimed to be excited, the level of their anticipation and happiness didn't measure up to my expectations—not by a long shot. Whenever I thought of my in-laws, a little wall of disappointment started to form around my heart.

Then, shortly before our son was born, I set up the nursery. Both Garret and I were so excited to welcome Jacob home to a loving, warm place. I had no idea that it would drive a wedge between me and my husband, as well as between him and my parents, to ask my father to help wallpaper and build a shelf for Jake's room. Dad had a lot of experience putting up borders and was great with woodworking; he and Mom knocked the work out in a few hours, and it looked fantastic.

I never imagined that when Garret came home, the changes in our house would make him feel angry, disrespected, and helpless. After some very heated words from him and a rather defensive series of comebacks from me, I realized that it wasn't so much that the work was done; it had nothing to do with how it looked. Garret simply felt he had no say in the matter. The decisions had been made without him, and I had looked to my parents—instead of him—for help. Feeling supplanted infuriated my husband. He never said one word to my parents, but hurt and frustration hung between them.

Fortunately, that memory faded into the distance. Things seemed to return to normal, and the day finally arrived for our baby boy to be delivered. Garret called his parents and told them to get in their car and start on their way to the hospital. The drive would take six hours, so we called them right when I went into labor. This should have given them plenty of time to see their grandson brought into this world. More than eight hours later, they showed up, missing Jacob's birth by over an hour. I seethed after discovering their tardiness wasn't due to traffic or weather or any other insurmountable odd. They didn't even seem sorry; they had just taken their time to get ready, unapologetically missing our little boy being born. The wall of disillusionment around my heart grew . . . and hardened.

Looking back, I can see that I had pretty fierce expectations for both sets of grandparents concerning their new grandchild. I assumed, for instance, that no matter what, they would drop everything and come running when we needed them. My parents had done this for my siblings and their kids—to me it seemed the "right" way to treat your children and grandchildren. Of course, this turned out to be an unrealistic expectation on many fronts. At times I realized that and let little disappointments slide, but other times, the grief and frustration I felt continued building that bitter wall around my heart.

As the years progressed, I became more and more disillusioned about becoming one big happy family. Spoken and unspoken expectations went unmet. Both my folks, who didn't seem to want to pursue a friendship with my in-laws, and Garret's folks, who didn't live up to my grandparenting hopes, chipped away at my dream. It seemed that not even Garret and I could stay a happy family. We didn't always see eye to eye, we often wounded each other, and I became more and more bitter (though I hid it quite convincingly!).

After nine years of marriage, my husband and I began a two-year journey through some very painful, hard times. During this period, the last remnants of my dream that we'd be one big happy family completely crumbled. My relationship with Garret's family crashed and burned. After a major heart attack, my dad—only sixty-seven years old—was suddenly taken home by the Lord.

I tried to talk to my husband about my disappointment, about my concern that we'd never be a happy family. Unfortunately, Garret and I didn't communicate well. Bringing up any shortcomings (perceived or otherwise) we saw in one another, or in each other's parents, was a recipe for anger, resistance, and all-out disaster.

I found myself venting to my family members instead of talking with Garret. Though I thought talking with my mom and siblings during our challenging times would help, it sometimes hurt everyone involved. Certain things my mother and brothers just couldn't understand; they often became irrationally angry at my husband. As Garret and I made decisions they disagreed with, it drove wedges between my family, Garret, and me. There were many horrible moments, many cruel words spoken. The fallout still affects me.

Thankfully—a trite word perhaps, but the best one I've got—the

Lord stood with us; each step of the way, through all our troubles and disappointments, He walked alongside. Through the Spirit's gentle nudgings, the people Jesus brought into our lives, prayer, and times in the Bible, the Lord revealed how unrealistic aspects of the "happy family" dream had poisoned my life and marriage.

Over time, I identified and confronted the bitterness toward my in-laws and the heartache in my own family, thus allowing closed doors to begin the slow process of opening again. I also began to acknowledge the negativity of my unspoken expectations as well as learned how to handle assumptions that went unfulfilled. Through the gift of asking forgiveness, I began to see myself, my marriage, and our entire extended family in a new light.

Today, I no longer cling to the overblown expectations about being one big happy family. I don't believe it's wrong or misguided to hope that your parents and in-laws will get along, nor is it bad to work toward building a healthy, vibrant relationship with the family you've been given, along with the one you marry into. In fact, these are great and important things to do.

But accepting that a good part of my "happily ever after" dream was idealistic and unrealistic has given me great freedom. I have learned to accept both our families' limitations and strengths. I have learned about my own boundaries and that my expectations aren't always the best; it would be impossible for anyone to fulfill them all.

There are still times when the sting of disappointment threatens me, when bitterness seems at the ready, eager to erect the walls around my heart once again. But I've learned to identify when my expectations aren't being met, turn them over to God (who is the only One who can carry them anyway), and be equipped by Him to love and forgive.

The Rules We Live By

My friend Melody learned, often through much pain and suffering, something we all intuitively sense: Everyone lives by a set of rules. Most people don't think of their expectations or preferences in those terms, but that's what they boil down to. Through our upbringing and the experiences of our lives, we come to think there are certain ways life *should* be lived, certain things that *shouldn't* been done. Not only does every individual move through life with an established — if not verbalized — set of assumptions but every family also operates with its own ideas of what's acceptable (and what's not).

Sadly but truly, the deeply entrenched "rules" we live by often wreak havoc on our relationships. Like Melody, many of us enter or look forward to marriage thinking everything will work out fine — we'll be the happiest family on the block! When the rules that guide our lives clash with someone else's, we often believe it's the other person's problem. If only he lived the "right" way, there'd be no issue.

It complicates matters further that marriage is not merely the blending of two lives; it's also the enmeshing of two families' ways of doing things — with all their (often eccentric) ideas about what's right and good. If you think your family doesn't have its quirks, think again. If you're aware of the unique ways your family views certain things or activities, great! You may have an easier time discerning what's negotiable and what's essential about "your way" of doing things.

Evaluating the rules you live by and the regulations that guide the people you love is part of maturity and growth. Melody discovered that one of her rules concerned grandparents: According to her, parents should always drop everything to help their children and grandchildren. By failing to abide by this unspoken rule, Melody's in-laws wounded her deeply. Over time, she allowed bitterness to take root, and walls of resentment began to form.

Melody's husband, Garret, wanted to have a say in his son's nursery and felt disrespected by Melody's spontaneous decision to ask her parents for help. To Garret, this signaled Melody's disloyalty to him and greater allegiance to her parents. Though this was in no way what Melody planned or desired, Garret felt hurt and frustrated by her decision.

As Garret and Melody's story demonstrates, the guidelines — or regulations we live by, depending upon how strictly an individual expects adherence to them — are rarely verbalized. They are always, however, *firmly established*. Needless to say, when a spouse, or any family member, breaks an unspoken rule, we often become much more vocal. Either that or we begin to shut down, surrendering to the creeping tide of bitterness.

Though they may be obvious to the person who's developed them, someone else's expectations for how things should be done may not be easy for you to identify. Rules for living can take many diverse forms. To illustrate the ways different kinds of rules influence daily life and relationships, I'd like to share a sampling of the expectations best-selling authors and psychologists Les and Leslie Parrott have encountered during their years of counseling singles and married couples:

- Don't interrupt another's work.
- Always buy organic fruits and vegetables.
- Don't ask for help unless you are desperate.
- Downplay your successes.
- Always leave the butter on the counter (not in the fridge).
- Don't work too long or too hard.
- Celebrate birthdays in a big way.
- Never raise your voice.
- Don't talk about your body.
- Always be on time.
- Clean the kitchen before you go to bed.
- Don't talk about your feelings.

- Always pay bills the day they arrive.
- Don't drive fast.
- Never buy dessert at a restaurant.
- Use a credit card only in an emergency.
- Don't buy expensive gifts.[1]

To you, some of these "rules" may seem ridiculous or confining, others important and essential. Perhaps you were raised with extravagant birthday parties and costly presents. If your spouse's family lived by the unspoken rule that expensive gifts are wasteful, however, trouble might be brewing.

The point is, we evaluate any stipulation—even this composite list of other couples' regulations—by *our own set* of rules. If we've never thought it mattered where the butter went, our spouse's unspoken expectation about where it belongs might strike us as silly or frustrating. But to the spouse raised in a particular "butter goes here" way, your reaction could feel demeaning or aggressive.

Here's one of the most important lessons we can learn before we marry, or at any stage of life we're currently in: We are free to accept *or* reject, challenge *and* change any rule, but only if we're doing it for the sake of relationship-building. If we're trying to force our way, if we're pursuing destructive means to make our rules everyone's rules, we go wrong. But if we're altering and amending guidelines we grew up with in order to better love and serve those around us, we are not only free, but sometimes obligated by the law of love, to do so.

In reading Garret and Melody's story, it's easy to see how unspoken rules and unverbalized expectations can drive wedges between family members and spouses. And my friends certainly aren't alone in what they faced. In fact, according to Drs. Dan Allender and Tremper Longman III, "The failure to shift loyalty from parents to spouse is a central issue in almost all marital conflict."[2] Fascinatingly and heartbreakingly, any sign that loyalty has not been transferred from "old family" to "new family" rules—whether this failure is perceived or actual—can seriously wound a spouse.

Carefully assessing and *communicating* which rules you deem nonnegotiable can only help you love those around you better. At times you may discover that a rule you once held dear is actually unrealistic and unhelpful. As it was for Melody, letting go of such regulations can be incredibly freeing. At other times you may need to help the people you love understand why and how a particular rule is important.

Popular Christian author H. Norman Wright, in his book *Now That You're Engaged,* offered three helpful responses a person can give after an expectation is vocalized. He urged us to use one of the following:

> 1. *"I can meet this expectation most of the time and I appreciate knowing about this. Can you tell me why this is important to you?"*
> 2. *"I can meet this expectation some of the time and I appreciate knowing about this. Can you tell me why this is important to you? How can I share with you when I cannot meet this so it would be acceptable to you?"*
> 3. *"This expectation would be difficult for me to meet for these reasons: _____. Can you tell me why this is so important to you? How will this affect you? How can some adjustments be worked out?"*[3]

Remember, for each of these three, some level of understanding regarding the other person's rule is essential, so if you still don't get why this is so important to the person/people you love, keep the dialogue going. Once some understanding has been gained, you can honestly evaluate if, how, and when you might be able to fulfill their expectation.

During a particularly challenging time for Jeramy and me (I had just suffered severe postpartum depression and was having a difficult time communicating to Jeramy how much my life had changed), we sought the counsel of a godly woman named Dr. Arlys McDonald.

When Jeramy and I expected or hoped for something, Dr. McDonald taught us how to make "behavior requests" rather than demands. To help us comprehend this concept, she likened marriage to neighbors living side by side, each with their own yard. One neighbor does not have the right to tromp over to the other's house and demand that a particular tree be cut down. Even if the tree seems to be causing problems between the neighbors—cracks in the sidewalk, perhaps—demanding or forcing your way will *never* yield positive results. The other neighbor will likely feel defensive and angry; he or she may even decide to keep the tree out of spite. Of course, this reaction would not be justified—malice is never permissible for those who live under God's love. His or her response, however, would be understandable, based on the method used by the other neighbor to effect change.

Fierce insistence doesn't work, but making behavior requests often does. Approaching someone you love with gentleness and respect, then asking that person to join you in holding to a certain rule or regulation provides far better—and longer-lasting—results than making a demand. Not only will the person feel he or she has a choice in the matter, but making that choice in the positive allows that person to take ownership and responsibility over the long haul.

For further application, let's apply this idea to one of the rules mentioned earlier: use credit cards only for emergencies. Say a husband notices his wife is spending somewhat recklessly on their shared credit card. She may even be endangering the family's finances (like an overgrown tree cracking the sidewalk).

It will do little good for the husband to "cut the tree down," approaching his wife with anger, resentment, and demands. If the situation is reversed, and the husband is the irresponsible spender, a wife may attempt to use manipulation, begging, or other backdoor means of demanding. But none of these methods would foster open and honest *dialogue* between the partners.

With healthy communication, however, behavior requests could be made: "Do you think we could both agree not to spend a certain amount without talking to each other?" Most reasonable people would concede this is a good policy to have, especially for married couples with financial concerns. If the spendy spouse concurs, the next step might be to express, "Great! That will really help us," and then ask, "What do you think a reasonable limit should be?"

Obviously, this is an artificially constructed dialogue, and marriages rarely find talks about finances, sex, in-laws, or other touchy subjects going quite so smoothly. There is hope, however, when we treat the people we love with respect and humility, requesting—but not demanding—that they understand and work with, even if they cannot perpetually meet, our expectations.

If you would like to build a happy family, perhaps a happy marriage, learning to evaluate the rules you live by, as well as how to communicate your hopes appropriately, really is important. It may not always be possible for two significantly different families to blend together in perfect harmony. Your parents and your in-laws may not be best friends. You may find some of the rules your spouse grew up with absolutely maddening. Even so, no one has to be an enemy. I urge you as Paul did the Romans, "Do your part to live in peace with everyone, as much as possible" (Romans 12:18, NLT).

As I'm sure you can imagine, learning more about how to communicate is key in the process of living in peace. Let's turn our attention now to some other aspects of the delicate art of communication.

Who? When? and How?

Scores of books have been written about communication. Many of them are truly amazing resources, helpful for singles and married couples. Consequently, I won't attempt to retread the ground that others have gone over.

Instead, I would like to focus on offering a few practical tips for learning to communicate about two essential things: your expectations and assumptions. That is the topic of our journey, and starting with the three little questions in the subtitle of this section, I encourage you to begin any conversation about hopes and rules by asking yourself these questions:

- Who is involved with this communication?
- When are we communicating?
- How are we communicating?

Though it seems simple, pausing to take stock of who, when, and how can make all the difference in a conversation about expectations.

The "who" question concerns knowing more than the names of the people involved (one of them is you, after all!); it centers on more than simply knowing *about* the person. Knowing "who is communicating" actually involves an accurate and loving appraisal of what the people communicating are like: What kind of temperament do they have? How do they react to criticism or encouragement? What preferences or aversions might need to be taken into consideration?

Lest you get discouraged, let me tell you up front: You don't have to spend hours and hours analyzing this. You may *want* to, and that is fine, as long as you are not making another person wait interminably. You can, however, rather quickly evaluate these matters, especially if you have taken opportunities beforehand to observe and get to know yourself and the people you love.

Identifying the "when" of communication is also critical. This, as with the "who," involves some honest evaluation: When would it be appropriate to talk about these things? When might the person I love be most responsive to my behavior request? When would the communication I hope for *not* go as well as I might desire? Looking at these issues will help any communication about expectations get off to a better start.

For me, talking late at night is *not* a good idea. I'm an early-to-bed, early-to-rise kind of girl, and I now know that late-night talks usually dissolve into arguments, even if neither Jeramy nor I intended it. I'm much better equipped to listen to Jeramy's communication if we talk when I'm rested and at full mental capacity (though I have to be honest . . . after kids, that seems like a rarity!).

In life, there will be times when discussing expectations won't be appropriate. Forcing a conversation in instances like those will only serve to harm (rather than help) a relationship. For example, right before Thanksgiving dinner at your in-laws' is probably not the best time to talk about your disappointment with their involvement in your life or in the lives of your kids. As much as possible—we all know that some conversations just happen at the wrong time, despite our best intentions—recognizing when to communicate is of central importance.

Jesus was a master communicator, and He clearly understood the importance of knowing *whom* He was speaking to, as well as *when* to bring things up. An excellent example of this comes in John 21. In this chapter, we find that, after denying he even knew Jesus (see John 18:15-27), Peter decided to return to his old life—that of a fisherman. Some of the other disciples opted to go with him.

According to John 21:3-5, a long (probably cold) night of fishing ended with the disciples clutching a dismally empty net. Just then, a stranger on the beach directed them to cast "off the right side of the boat. . . . All of a sudden there were so many fish in [the net], they weren't strong enough to pull it in. . . . When Simon Peter realized that it was the Master, he threw on some clothes, for he was stripped for work, and dove into the sea" (verses 6-7). Arriving on the shore, dripping wet, Peter was warmed by the fire Jesus had been tending. He and the other disciples were nourished by the fish Jesus had prepared for breakfast. And only after these physical needs were met did Jesus confront Peter with his responsibilities to shepherd and feed the flock of God (see verses 15-17).

I love this account for so many reasons, but Peter's fiery passion — exemplified by his impetuous dive into the Sea of Galilee — is definitely at the top of my list. Jesus knew Peter's zeal for Him; He also knew the cowardice that prompted Peter to deny his Lord. Jesus knew *whom* He was speaking to when He asked Peter three times, "Do you love me?" (verses 15-17). Jesus also knew *when* to communicate with Peter. Our Lord graciously took the time to warm and feed His disciple before challenging him.

Of course, we will never perfectly understand our loved ones, definitely not in the way Jesus understood Peter! But we *can* take the time to evaluate whom we're talking with — what defines them, what moves them, what changes them. Similarly, though we won't have Christ's impeccable timing, we *can* slow down, analyze the circumstances, and wait if necessary. Like Jesus modeled for us, we can take steps to meet the timely needs that will best enable us and our loved ones to communicate.[4]

And finally we come to the "how." It's the "how" that often trips us up, isn't it? It's the "how" that has spawned millions of copies of books, DVDs, and lectures on communication. Again, we'll restrict ourselves to exploring only "how to communicate your expectations." This will help us focus a huge and never-ending topic.

When it comes to communicating your hopes and assumptions, I'd like to teach (or remind you of) two basic principles:

1. Use "I," not "you," statements.
2. Practice mirroring.

If you can develop skills in these two areas, you can avoid the majority of problems people encounter when communicating their expectations.

Using "I" statements sounds simple, but carrying it out is often more difficult than we realize. It's *so easy* to launch into "but you did this" or "but you said that . . . " conversations. You may have heard that using "I" sentences keeps the person you're communicating with from defensiveness. You may know that avoiding "you" statements helps people assume personal responsibility for what they can and should. (Very, very rarely in marriage is one person absolutely right and the other absolutely wrong.) But I ask you, are you actually *practicing* this technique?

If you've never heard the difference between an "I" and "you" statement, let me give you an example and brief explanation. An "I" statement regarding expectations might sound something like this: "I would like for us to consider using our Saturdays as a work-around-the-house day. There are a lot of projects I'd like to tackle, and it would be great to work on them together."

A "you" statement would sound quite different: "The house is falling apart, and you and I have a lot to get done. You should plan to keep Saturdays free for the next couple of months." If the conversation is a particularly heated one, a "you" sentence may be even more aggressive: "You never do anything around the house, and look at the state it's in! You'd better stay home on Saturday, or else I'll hire a contractor, and that will mean we can kiss this year's vacation good-bye."

Do you see how the latter two statements differ from the first?

Again, matters of respect and gentleness are at stake. Though it may be difficult, try to use "I" statements as much as possible. With practice, this does become more natural. It may feel awkward and frustrating at first (especially if you passionately believe you are in the right), but developing this skill is crucial, whether or not you are married.

Learning to mirror (or to practice reflective listening, as some psychologists call it) is another life skill that you can take into marriage or keep with you in singlehood. Along with instructing us in the art of behavior requests, Dr. McDonald also helped Jeramy and me build up our skills in this area. Mirroring, or reflective listening, involves repeating back the communication you receive. It also includes setting aside focused time for each partner to have his or her say, without interruption by the other communicator.

If you were to practice this skill with regard to an expectation, your conversation might follow a pattern like this: The people communicating would decide who will go first and who will mirror. If an agreement cannot be found on this matter, taking a break until tempers are less heated might be wise.

The person who will communicate first then uses "I" statements to articulate what he or she feels, believes, and hopes for. Without interrupting, and with as little "thinking what I am going to say next" as possible, the person listening waits until the communicator stops. The listener then asks, "Is that all you would like to say?" The other person responds yes or no, depending on the situation.

The listener then mirrors back what he or she has just heard and understood from the other person, also using "I" statements. (For instance, "I hear you saying that you would like to work around the house together for the next few weeks. I hear that this is very important to you.") The listener always closes his or her mirroring with the question, "Have I received your communication correctly?" If so, the partners take a break and come together after a few minutes to switch roles.

If not, the communicator takes a few moments to clarify anything that may have been misperceived. When the roles are reversed, the conversation follows the same course.

As far as ground rules for mirroring go, there are only a few: Use "I" statements, listen attentively, do your best to communicate back what you've heard, and take only the time you require (in other words, don't overrun your partner by talking endlessly; if you need help with this, consider using a timer for ten-, fifteen-, or twenty-minute intervals). Remember, you can always switch roles again if a first round of mirroring doesn't end with understanding.

Mirroring is a very powerful communication tool but one that many couples refuse to use. Perhaps it seems too awkward or extensive a process for them. However, those who don't learn to mirror miss out on a technique that genuinely helps people arrive at mutual understanding. Remember, "fools think they need no advice, but the wise listen to others" (Proverbs 12:15, NLT).

I urge you: Don't wait until marriage to practice mirroring. Parents and children can listen reflectively, brothers and sisters, friends, colleagues—you name it. The key is to press through the initial moments of feeling disconcerted. We are so used to interrupting, sadly accustomed to running over each other. It is different, indeed, to *listen* and to reflect. But wisdom calls us to listen, and in listening we find our relationships strengthened and more of our expectations fulfilled or appropriately reordered.

Most people, married or single, would like to have healthier interactions with the people they're around, day in and day out. But as we've seen, building healthy, godly relationships requires a good deal of effort. Developing communication skills like those explored in this chapter is part of the work required of anyone who wishes to mature. If you want good familial relationships (today or someday), invest your time in communicating well.

Still, I should warn you that not even good communication can *guarantee* that everyone in your family will get along (or that you'll have the kind of "happy family" you hope for). You can take responsibility before you marry, or at whatever stage you currently are, to establish healthy channels of communication. The people you interact with, however, will make their own decisions, some of which may sabotage your relationships.

Indeed, in our efforts to communicate with others, we are often forced to confront the bitterness and resentment that can so easily weasel into relationships, whether with a spouse or anyone else. When faced with the hurts of our past and the wounds of our present, there is really only one place to turn . . .

Forgiveness

In intimate relationships, conflict is natural.

No, it's more than that: It's *unavoidable.*

In life, we wound the people we love; they wound us. There's just no way around it.

If you marry, the spouse you choose *will* hurt you—deeply. The wounds may be more frequent or less, depending on your own maturity and that of the person you marry. But no one you know—including yourself—will be perfect this side of heaven. You can count on needing to forgive.

Whether or not you marry, the hurts people you love inflict on you, as well as those you inflict on others, will cry out for healing. When confronted with this pain, you have two choices: to bury your pain or forgive the wrongs. But be warned: If you bury a wound, you bury it alive. It will claw its way out of your heart and through your mind, slowly poisoning you with bitterness and resentment.

Forgiveness is the way of freedom, the way of life. And for Christians, forgiveness is really the *only* option—"You *must* make allowance for each other's faults and forgive the person who offends you. Remember, the Lord forgave you, so you *must* forgive others" (Colossians 3:13, NLT, emphasis added). God offers no "plan B." To know Him and be counted with His Son, we must be forgiven. To grow in His likeness, we must forgive. This is His design—perfect, lasting, and true.

In her journey, Melody discovered the amazing power, as well as the genuine necessity, of forgiveness. Both her husband and the extended family around her needed her forgiveness, as well as to extend forgiveness to one another. This is the fundamental story of each of our lives. When it comes to forgiveness, the questions most people have aren't about whether or not it's necessary. Most people—even nonbelievers—see that they hurt and have been hurt. They also see that something is needed to deal with the pain. For most of us, the difficulties come in knowing *how* to forgive and what genuine forgiveness looks like.

Fortunately, the Bible answers the question of how to forgive. The New American Standard Bible renders the latter half of Colossians 3:13, "Just as the Lord forgave you, so also should you."

Just as the Lord forgave . . .

Well, there's our answer. But it's not one we can grasp easily, let alone apply. God's forgiveness of us—among other things—is wholesale, complete, and eternal. So often we forgive conditionally ("I'll forgive him if and when he . . ."), halfheartedly ("he'll only do it again . . . I don't know why I even bother"), and for less time than it takes to snatch our pain back from the Lord and the person who hurt us. I don't know about you, but I'm not so great at forgiving forever.

Sometimes, the sorrow of a past wound will come to me again and again, like waves of fury and agony crashing on the shore of my heart. I used to think that any time I felt the pain of a former hurt again, it meant I had failed to forgive at all. But experience and time have taught me to recognize that these waves of grief are God's blessing, a chance for me to go deeper and higher with Him into the grace of forgiveness.

The Lord can forgive all at once, in a wipe-the-slate-clean kind of way. Our limited human minds, however, can process only portions of anguish at a time. Forgiveness is a process for us on earth, *not* a one-time event. It's something that unfolds . . . and enfolds. As forgiveness opens up within us, love and mercy surround us — slowly, but certainly, setting us free. The ache of past wounds has little power over the heart that chooses forgiveness.

I appreciate how Douglas Weiss described forgiveness in his very practical book *The Ten-Minute Marriage Principle*. Weiss observed, "Forgiveness is a gift you give to yourself. This gift allows you to disconnect from the perpetrator and the pain [to] release them from your heart so you can heal."[5]

In a similar vein, Lewis Smedes, a brilliant theologian and author of two of the best books on forgiveness available in print, called forgiveness spiritual surgery *on your own soul.* In *The Art of Forgiving,* Smedes wrote, "The first and sometimes only person to get the benefits of forgiving is the person who does the forgiving."[6] Like a tourniquet that stops the bleeding of *your* own heart, a medicine that prevents *your* heart from becoming poisoned by bitterness and resentment, forgiveness heals and sets you free.

Despite what many people believe or try to practice, forgiveness is not about forgetting the wounds of our past. Instead, we learn to *remember redemptively,* to let the memories of our former wounds be progressively lost in the same Love who forgave us. Forgiveness is also not about immediately letting the person who hurt us back into our lives. Forgiveness is between you and God; reconciliation is between you and the person who offended you (or whom you offended). This takes time, honesty on the part of both parties, and a willingness to change.

Sadly, there are times when reconciliation is not viable. Forgiveness, however, is always possible.

Over the course of your life, the disappointment of unfulfilled expectations will either draw you to forgiveness or drive you to madness. I pray that you would be wooed by the forgiving Love who saves, rather than driven by the harsh masters of bitterness and resentment.

A lot is up to you, however; forgiveness begins with a choice, a choice that sometimes must be made over and over again. Whether or not the person who hurt you ever says sorry, whether or not a person from whom you ask forgiveness ever extends it, you can choose to walk through the pain and be released from it. You can be free.

If forgiveness is a challenging subject for you (and it is for most of us), I urge you to dialogue with the Lord about your struggles and to listen for His wisdom through whatever source He chooses to communicate. Learning to authentically forgive is a skill that each of us desperately needs, and I have personally grown through studying and writing about this important topic.[7] Forgiveness is one of the most significant parts of a healthy marriage. Whether or not you're currently married, start practicing now, letting God show you how free you can be.

Pressing On . . .

1. In this chapter, we explored the idea that people have various rules by which they live. What would a list of your rules look like? Which of your regulations are negotiable, and which are nonnegotiable? How could you communicate the most important rules in your life to a loved one who might struggle to understand some of the guidelines you live by? Now read Colossians 2:16-18,20-23:

So don't let anyone condemn you for what you eat or drink, or for not celebrating certain holy days or new-moon ceremonies or Sabbaths. For these rules were only shadows of the real thing, Christ himself. Don't let anyone condemn you by insisting on self-denial. . . .

You have died with Christ, and he has set you free from the evil powers of this world. So why do you keep on following rules of the world, such as, "Don't handle, don't eat, don't touch." Such rules are mere human teaching about things that are gone as soon as we use them. These rules may seem wise because they require strong devotion, humility, and severe bodily discipline. But they have no effect when it comes to conquering a person's evil thoughts and desires. (NLT)

What do these verses teach us about some of the rules we make? Based on what you've read, are there any personal or familial regulations you want to rethink or discard?

2. According to some research, effective communication consists of 7 percent content, 38 percent tone of voice, and 55 percent nonverbal communication.[8] For me, this statistic was a startling surprise. I knew that tone of voice and nonverbal cues were important, but I wouldn't have guessed that they make up 93 percent of what we communicate. How does this revelation strike you? How might the decision to change your tone of voice, unfold your arms, or send any number of other nonverbal signals change a negative conversation into a more positive one? If you are a dramatic person, in what ways would choosing a tone of voice and set of nonverbal signs that communicate balance and perspective help someone to understand you better, even if you *are* feverishly passionate—hurt, angry, confused, or overjoyed—about something? If you are a nonemotive

person, what compromises in tone and nonverbal signals might you make to help your loved ones feel more welcome to express their ideas?

3. According to Scripture, wisdom and understanding come through listening to and heeding constructive correction; refusing to listen leads to destruction. Proverbs 15:31-32 reveals, "If you listen to constructive criticism, you will be at home among the wise. If you reject criticism, you only harm yourself; but if you listen to correction, you grow in understanding" (NLT). How skilled are you at listening well? How quick are you to take the constructive counsel of others? If this is not your strong suit, what would it take for you to grow in this area? If this is something you do well, how can you help others mature?

4. Christian counselors often (and wisely!) remind people to cultivate genuine empathy in listening. With empathy comes the willingness to change. It's not enough to learn to listen well; often we are called to act on what we've heard. Drs. Les and Leslie Parrott wisely recommend that if a person you love makes a behavior request, you seriously consider his or her desire; if it seems feasible, act on it.[9] Think of the last time someone made a behavior request of you. How did you respond? If you reacted poorly, what could you have done differently? How might reflective listening and empathetic action have changed a negative situation into a more positive one?

5. In the section on forgiveness, we looked at Colossians 3:13, which urges us to forgive others as God has forgiven us. In the book of Ephesians, the Lord issues a similar command: "Get rid of all bitterness, rage, anger, harsh words, and slander, as well as all types of malicious behavior. Instead, be kind to each other, tenderhearted,

forgiving one another, just as God through Christ has forgiven you" (4:31-32, NLT). As we all know, anger, bitterness, and gossip often come with deep wounds. Think of a particular instance in which forgiveness has been difficult for you to extend, a circumstance in which you may have been hardhearted rather than tenderhearted toward a person or people who wronged you. According to the ideas we explored, why would forgiving the person/people from whom you've withheld forgiveness not only be the *right* thing to do but the *shrewd* thing as well? How might forgiveness—"spiritual surgery on your own soul"—help to heal and restore you? For what anger, bitterness, and malicious behavior might you want to ask forgiveness?

TEN

It Will Be Forever

I remember the very moment I knew in the deepest part of my heart that my marriage was over. It was when Dave moved out. I was in the shower, and he was leaving. I was half-moaning, half-crying, wailing from a deep, guttural place of my being. It was the sound of utter heartbreak . . . of a million dreams crashing down around me.

—DANIELLE WHITNEY

WHAT HAPPENS TO A woman who finally gets married, only to watch the dreams she's cherished—the "till death do us part" hopes—shatter? What goes on in the heart of a woman who finds herself unexpectedly single again?

Have you ever imagined yourself widowed or separated, annulled or divorced?

If you're anything like me, these are circumstances you don't even *want* to consider. Indeed, for our first dance as a married couple, Jeramy and I waltzed to an old standard that captured my heart's cry: "When I fall in love, it will be forever, or I'll never fall in love." Forever . . . that's a long time and a pretty tall order, if you think about it. But I fully anticipate and expect nothing less from my marriage—give me a love that lasts, or count me out.

Many of you are with me, I know. Since childhood, you've hoped for a "happily ever after" that lasts . . . *ever after.* Even if you came from a broken home, did your heart long for this kind of love?

"When I get married, it will be forever . . ."

A book like this could never be complete without addressing this assumption. But such an expectation is one of the most heartbreaking and problematic to explore. The issues surrounding enduring marriages are complex and thorny enough, but add the dynamics of separation, death, and divorce to the mix, and you've got a veritable powder keg of complications.

Part of my difficulty in discussing these issues comes from the fact that I am writing primarily for singles and for couples who are still together. I do not, therefore, plan to provide advice in this chapter for those currently going through the heart-wrenching experiences of grief, divorce, or separation. If you are in such a situation, there are some wonderful, Christ-centered resources available.[1] In this book, I hope to help prepare your heart for whatever you might face in the future, whether that be continued singlehood, a marriage that lasts, or one that ends for some reason or another.

To help us begin navigating such difficult terrain, I asked a dear friend and amazing woman of God to share her experience with you.

Faithful and True
As told by Danielle Whitney

Dave and I heard about each other for six years before officially meeting. Both professional counselors in Chicago's metro area, we shared several mutual friends and colleagues. We also spoke at the same singles' conferences on more than one occasion, though even working so closely we never came face-to-face. When a girlfriend of mine who worked with Dave finally concocted a plan to introduce us and see if there might be a connection, it seemed an exciting possibility.

After a year of casual friendship, Dave and I began dating. Our courtship proceeded quickly, and after five months, I found myself engaged, happily awaiting a wedding less than two months away. I felt I knew Dave pretty well. And at thirty-three myself, with Dave nearing forty-three, there seemed little reason to draw out our dating or engagement.

From the outset, it appeared Dave and I knew more about marriage than your average couple. Both of us had extensive instruction in marital therapy through our counseling courses. While studying for my master's, I also took some wonderful classes on male/female dynamics and the biblical blueprint for marriage. I went through church training for premarital counseling and learned to administer tests that not only highlighted a couple's strengths and weaknesses but also helped me address these areas with them. I read scads of books and amassed a small library dealing with various aspects of marriage, from conflict resolution to healthy sexuality. One would think Dave and I were more than prepared to tackle marriage.

Of course, I knew that difficulties inherently come with any intimate relationship, but I still imagined Dave would be my best friend and lover. I eagerly anticipated that our emotional and sexual connection would be intimate, fulfilling, and faithful. And I assumed that Dave would be the leader of our relationship and home, a man of honor and integrity, a man whose word was his bond. I genuinely believed we would go the distance together.

The reality that our marriage wouldn't be all I hoped for hit me our very first night as husband and wife. Dave took me to an actual castle for our first night together. I remember being so excited for us to finally come together as "one." Nervous but thrilled, I changed in the bathroom for our big night, fully expecting his look of enjoyment as I presented myself to him. I came out of the bathroom dressed in a pearl-colored nightgown, genuinely feeling beautiful.

It's hard to describe the pain and confusion that descended when, as if refusing to really look at me, Dave quickly shut his eyes and began mechanically kissing my lips. I longed for him to drink in the sight of me, to enjoy the gift I offered him. But there was nothing romantic or intimate about his gaze, his touch. Instead, it felt that night like Dave was trying to play a role he thought he "should." Nothing in those first few moments communicated that he really wanted me.

The fact that Dave was impotent and we were unable to have sex for most of our honeymoon didn't help matters. Neither did the persistence of this problem. A year later, when we came back to that same castle to celebrate our one-year anniversary, I remember trying and trying to have sex until late into the night, to no avail. We both ended up sobbing in the Jacuzzi tub.

Since I've always been a "let it all hang out (and then some)" person, I talked and talked and talked with Dave about our problems. We went to marriage counseling so that we could really work on things. But instead of getting better, things started unraveling faster and more furiously.

The first time I caught Dave in a bold-faced lie will never leave my memory. He was at home one day, writing out checks for bills that needed to be paid. Before that day, I never doubted we were on the same financial page. Because we wanted to pay off the debt Dave incurred prior to our meeting, we had both agreed to account for every penny we spent, live within a careful budget, and cut up all credit cards. Since I was getting ready to head off for work, I picked up the stamped envelopes, offering to take out the mail for him. Dave quickly grabbed the stack out of my hands and said, "No, that's okay; I'll do it." Just then, something fell to the floor: a blank money order. I asked, "What's this?" and Dave explained he got it to pay the annual fee for one of his professional organizations. Trusting him completely, I responded, "Oh, okay." But something nagged at me . . . why would he go to the trouble of getting a money order? When I asked him why he hadn't simply written a check, Dave replied, "I just wanted to do it this way." Though a bit perplexed by his response, I still believed my husband. When I asked him if it wouldn't be easier now to just write a check for the amount, he snipped, "I want to handle it this way." Dave's answers didn't make sense. And then, it dawned on me . . . no, it actually hit me like a load of bricks — Dave was lying.

This might seem obvious in the retelling, but I had never thought until that moment that my husband would lie to me. I turned to him and asked, "What is this for, Dave?" Again he claimed it was for the annual fee. At that point he knew I didn't believe him. Again I asked him what it was for. Again he gave the same answer. We stood there, staring at each other in the kitchen, my heart sinking like lead into my stomach.

"You're lying to me!" I exclaimed. Dave denied it. "You are looking straight into my eyes and lying!" I pressed. Dumbfounded, shocked beyond reason that my husband would tell a bold-faced lie right to my face, I stood there, peering into his eyes, silent as the grave.

After what seemed like a long time, Dave confessed that the money was to pay for a credit card he had been using on the side, a card I didn't know anything about. Needless to say, I felt shocked, horrified, very angry, and deeply betrayed. I thought I had an honest partner, a teammate working with me on a mutual goal (debt reduction), when all the while he was incurring debt behind my back. Dismayed, I wondered how I ended up marrying someone dishonest. But if it was difficult for me to process this one lie, it was infinitely more painful to learn that my husband had woven his entire life in a web of deceit and duplicity.

When Dave was looking for a job, I found copies of résumés he sent out, boasting of degrees he never received and experiences he never had. Then, through a series of events only God could have orchestrated, I discovered the extent of his past experimentation with homosexuality.

During this time, I called two trusted friends, asking if they would begin praying that God would uncover anything else that was hidden. Though on one level I wanted these prayers to be answered, when God actually began unveiling layer after layer of Dave's deception, when my husband continued to get caught in one lie after another, all within a very short period, it nearly overwhelmed me.

It was hard for me to fathom the scope of his dishonesty. I felt deeply conned and completely baffled. Was I that blind? Was I that gullible? How could I miss something so big? Were there warning signs I had ignored or misread from the very beginning?

Through this period of unraveling, I was up, down, and inside out—all over the map emotionally, spiritually, and physically. At times I felt patient, surrendered, and at peace, bringing God my aching heart, pouring it into intercession, and giving Him what I knew I could neither control nor change. I fought so hard to let go of what I believed things "should" or "would" be. At other points, a raging, despairing hopelessness overtook me; there were moments I felt so ripped off by the whole situation, and even by God. Sometimes I shut down and withdrew; other times I cried oceans of tears. Ugliness and an angry demandingness I had never known erupted from within me. And at the same time, the physical exhaustion and depletion from not resting well for months on end started to catch up with me (suffering from sleep apnea, Dave snored severely and made it nearly impossible for me to sleep). Strange symptoms led one doctor to suspect I had MS. After an MRI ruled that out, it seemed clear that sleep deprivation and stress were responsible for some of my bizarre physiological reactions.

Not knowing who the person I married really was, I asked Dave to move out and temporarily separate. I needed him to decide if he was bent on living lies or wanted to move forward in truth. Our marriage could not continue if built on deception.

We were separated for eight months, during which we mostly wrote letters and spoke on the phone. Through that long string of days, God repeatedly said two things to me: "Do you trust Me?" and "Wait." I didn't know what I was waiting for, but I knew that until I sensed His clear leading, I wasn't to do anything about my marriage.

I spent hours and hours poring over the Scriptures on marriage and divorce. "What therefore God has joined together, let no man separate," Jesus commanded in Matthew 19:6 (NASB), and "I hate divorce," says the Lord in Malachi 2:16. From a variety of other passages, including Matthew 5, I knew I did not have biblical grounds to end the marriage. I suspected that Dave had been unfaithful to me but had no conclusive proof. At the end of those eight long months, Dave finally came clean, confessing the adulterous and homosexual encounters he had during our second year of marriage.

At that point, I truly felt released by God to seek a legal dissolution of our relationship, one that would reflect what actually happened—Dave never entered into the covenant of marriage with me. The day after what would have been our third anniversary, a judge granted our annulment.

Before I got married, I assumed that my husband would tell me the truth and that he would be sexually faithful to me, as he vowed on our wedding day. I still have hopes of being married again, and honestly, I would enter into any marriage with those same expectations. It's painful but important to recognize that even if our expectations are healthy and realistic—even biblical—God doesn't guarantee anyone a marriage that lasts forever. Dave and I both had the power of choice; we could decide to live out—or betray—our commitment.

I never imagined that I would be single again, especially not three years after my wedding day. But the older I get, the more I realize that while the life I have is not always the life I signed up for, planned out, or dreamed of, it's this painful gap between what I long for and what I actually live that reveals some of the deeper, darker places of my heart, places that God wants to cleanse and purify. It's this gap that brings an invitation to experientially know more of Jesus' love, filling me in the midst of unmet longings.

My heart was broken into a thousand pieces by all of this. But God took my heart and held it, breathing life and healing into places I thought would never be whole again. He's expanded my heart to contain more of His love. And through it all, He's proven Himself to be faithful and true.

When my husband was unfaithful, God was faithful. When my husband told me lie after lie, God continued to shelter me with His truth. If there's one thing God has shown me over and over again, so that I know it's true, it's that my God is faithful and true. I can bank on this for the rest of my life, whether I stay single or get married again.

I was single until age thirty-three and have been single again from age thirty-six until now (I'm forty-two). I've spent the majority of my life single, which is not what I wanted—and the desire to be married has never gone away. But like nothing else, singleness has caused me to seek and commune intimately with God.

Both "never been married" singleness and "my marriage is over" singleness have beckoned me to come to God. He's revealed that my longing to be married comes out of a deeper well, an ache within me to share unmatched intimacy with Him. He wants to be the primary longing of my heart, above my longing to be married, because He knows only His love is forever, only His love truly fulfills.

On a good day, I can remember this and am truly content. On a bad day, I can act like a pouting child, feeling ripped off, questioning God's way of doing things in my life. I'll be the first to admit that the endurance of my single station has instigated the fiercest wrestling in my soul with God. But without it, I could not have learned that only His love is perfectly faithful and true.

What Does He Guarantee?

Danielle shared something toward the end of her story that I'd like to revisit: "It's painful but important to recognize that even if our expectations are healthy and realistic—even biblical—God doesn't guarantee anyone a marriage that lasts forever."

How does that strike you? How does the idea that it's the "painful gap" between the life you're living and the life you planned for and dreamed of that actually reveals some of the places God most wants to heal and restore, cleanse and purify in your heart?

Like Danielle, the older I get, the more I acknowledge that life rarely (as in almost never) works out exactly as I planned. Whether or not they choose to recognize it, this is true for all men and women. It follows quite naturally, then, that the gap between what we desire and what actually happens widens and deepens the longer we live. And often, though it usually surprises us, what matters most is not what we hoped for, or even what really happened, but what we did with the gap.

It's in the gap that we choose to trust or to despair, to persevere or to give up. In the gap, we discover that our heartache can be healed, that our hopes can be restored. In the gap, we learn to say, "The LORD gave and the LORD has taken away. Blessed be the name of the LORD" (Job 1:21, NASB). *He* is in the gap.

I remember when, during the first couple of years of my marriage, a young woman in our church was suddenly widowed. In an instant, in an accident no one could have foreseen or planned for, her husband was taken from her forever. The ladies in our Bible study group talked about the reality that it could have happened to any one of us, but I recall thinking (perhaps in an attempt at self-consolation) that her husband was a pilot while mine was a pastor; surely my chances for such a tragedy were far less likely.

A short time later, a dear friend of ours lost a prolonged battle with breast cancer. She left a grieving husband and two heartbroken daughters. Not too long after that, a friend's husband, while coaching little league hockey, fell backward and hit his head on the ice rink floor. He died later that night. And these stories are just a few among many. I've been to the memorial services of more young spouses than I ever imagined. The gap between what we desire—a lifetime of married love—and what often happens—painful separation—is very real. It can rip open in any life.

At every funeral, at the table of every abandoned spouse whose partner walked out, there's someone wondering, "How can I be single again?" Standing at the altar, wide-eyed with the wonder of marriage, few people picture themselves facing a forced reentry into singlehood. But we know that today, roughly half of all marriages end in divorce. A large majority of the other half end in the death of one or both of the partners (the remaining relationships dissolving through annulment or other extenuating circumstances). Since couples don't usually pass away simultaneously, that means a high percentage of married people will—at some point in their lives—become single again.

I know it's neither comfortable nor preferable to think about, but to approach marriage in the healthiest way, we must realize that God doesn't guarantee us a marriage that lasts forever. What He *does* guarantee is that He will be with us forever. That's why the prophet Nehemiah urged us, "Stand up and praise the LORD your God, for he lives from everlasting to everlasting! . . . Praise his glorious name! It is far greater than we can think or say" (Nehemiah 9:5, NLT).

From everlasting to everlasting . . . *forever*! A spouse cannot be with you forever, but the Lord can. You may recall that we also explored this idea, albeit from some different angles, in chapter 4: "Life Will Be So Much Better."

As Psalm 103 reminds us,

> *Men and women don't live very long;*
> *like wildflowers they spring up and blossom,*
> *But a storm snuffs them out just as quickly,*

> *leaving nothing to show they were here.*
> GOD's *love, though, is ever and always,*
> *eternally present to all who fear him,*
> *Making everything right for them and their children.*
> (verses 15-17)

Not only does our Savior guarantee that He will be—ever and always—with us in the gap between what we hope for and what we have, but He also promises to help us endure the tumultuous emotions that flood us when we're there; that's why we can say "even when walking through the dark valley of death I will not be afraid, for you are close beside me, guarding, guiding all the way" (Psalm 23:4, TLB).

When fear and confusion, pain or depression threaten, you can cling to the truth that God is close beside you, guarding and guiding all the way. This is not just a nice saying, nor is it merely wishful thinking; this is the truth you must build your life on. We cannot focus our lives on or around marriage, but we *can* place our trust solidly in the One who is faithful and true. His guarantees to us are forever presence, forever love, forever hope. These are yours no matter what your station.

Wanted and Defended

Aside from the physical reality that death separates many married lovers, abandonment, undesired separation, or divorce may also drive a couple apart. Danielle certainly did not want to see her marriage break up. Indeed, the dissolution of a marriage often occurs despite the desire of one of the partners. An abandoned spouse (sometimes left with children to tend on her own) may face not only the painful gap between what she hoped for and what she has but also some difficult questions that cut to the core of who she is: Am I desirable? Am I lovable? Am I worth pursuing and protecting?

We spent a good deal of time at the beginning of the book talking about the crucial importance of answering such questions before one marries. Truly, if we haven't settled in our heart that we are cherished, valued, and loved beyond measure by One who will *never stop* loving us in this way, we will always be looking to our spouse to provide something that he can never give—security and confidence on the deepest level.

When a spouse is rejected or abandoned, not only can old questions like these resurface, but new questions can also arise. Aching doubt and profound confusion can nag at the heart of someone who feels suddenly discarded, unwanted, and unworthy.

Do you recall how Danielle wrote in her story about the grief of her wedding night, when Dave refused to truly *look* at her, when his touch failed to communicate longing desire for her? Women who've been abandoned or divorced often feel, in a similar way, that they've given the best they have, only to be rejected.

For Danielle, God wove a great story of redemption through the pain of feeling undesirable. She told me that sometime after she and Dave separated, God gave her an incredibly healing experience in prayer, which enabled her to tangibly sense her worth and value: Jesus was with her in her honeymoon suite. Taken with her heart, He wanted to gaze upon her and *could not* turn His eyes away. Though Danielle had felt "unseen" by Dave on her wedding night, the eternal Bridegroom revealed His deep desire and love for her.

A spouse may reject or abandon you, but your God will *never* turn away. Psalm 94:14 beautifully proclaims, "The Lord will not reject [you]; he will not abandon his own special possession" (NLT). You, His treasured one, will not be cast aside. "No," declares Romans 11:2, "God has not rejected his own people, whom he chose from the very beginning" (NLT). You have been chosen because you are dearly loved. No matter what may come in your future, no matter what a spouse may or may not do to you, you can bank on His everlasting love.

You can also trust that He will defend you. During divorce or abandonment, spouses often lie about one another. I sincerely hope you never have to endure this hardship, but if you do, I pray it will reveal to you that God is your defender.

The psalmist wrote, "The Lord is my rock, my protection, my Savior. My God is my rock. I can run to him for safety. He is my shield and my saving strength, my defender" (Psalm 18:2, NCV). Had David and the other psalmists never faced adversity—being betrayed, deceived, and lied about—how could they have known God as saving strength and defender? How can we know Him as defender if we need no defense?

Danielle told me that when she discovered Dave had lied to other people about their relationship, it was incredibly hard for her not to defend herself. She said that one of her pastors acted "as if [Danielle] had the plague" after she and Dave separated. Naturally, she wanted to set things straight and reestablish her reputation. But Danielle felt God entreating her to trust Him as her vindicator. Instead of pouring her energy into defending herself and following up on all of Dave's lies, trying to figure out where they ended, she invested time in getting to know God as her defender. According to Danielle, it was one of the hardest things she's done. But how can you put a price on being able to claim personally and confidently, "The LORD is *my* light and my salvation; whom shall I fear? The LORD is *the defense of my life*; whom shall I dread?" (Psalm 27:1, NASB, emphasis added).

We needn't spend pages and pages dissecting what might happen if a spouse abandons or rejects you. We'd be far better served to spend our time looking at God's character, for it is His faithful and true love, His wholesale acceptance of us, the value He places on us, and the promises He makes to defend and protect us that really count.

So I urge you, before you marry, or in whatever stage of marriage you currently are, to dive into the passages that reveal God as the One who desires and defends you. As you search the Scriptures and learn more of His heart, no matter what may pass in your single or married life, you will know the God whose rock-solid character will guard and guide you.

The Role of Your Choice

We've looked at the way death and unwanted separation can drive couples apart. But what happens to a spouse who expects his or her marriage to last forever, but then willingly and willfully chooses to end it?

Before we tackle a question of such magnitude, it's important to note that in this section, we will be dealing with a lot of difficult "gray" areas. Is it ever, for instance, biblically justifiable for a battered wife to seek divorce? Is the husband whose alcoholic wife slowly destroys their life, drinking their savings away and wreaking havoc in their home, required by God to "gut it out" and stay married no matter what? How should a woman whose husband has been sexually abusing their children deal with her spouse?

I do not have—and do not believe any human can offer—perfect answers for these horrible situations. And though, like Danielle, I unwaveringly believe that divorce is not God's desire for His children, there are still no perfect biblical formulas for living through the trauma of a marriage riddled with issues like domestic abuse, sexual addiction, or chemical dependency.

Most pastors and Bible teachers agree that in the sad instances where infidelity is present, the betrayed spouse has clear biblical grounds for divorce (see Matthew 5:31-32). Because of God's grace, every couple who faces the trauma of an affair must not necessarily choose to separate and dissolve their marriage. But when a spouse has been unfaithful, God does allow for divorce.

Yet what of the other instances we mentioned? What is God's good and perfect will (see Romans 12:2) for these circumstances? There are simply no black-and-white, cut-and-dried, "do this and you'll be in the center of God's will" answers. Instead, these are matters for discernment between individuals and the Holy Spirit within them.

God is always more interested in what's happening in the heart of a man or woman than in what's happening with his or her external behavior (see, for instance, the evidence for this in the Sermon on the Mount, Matthew 5–7). Of course, our actions absolutely matter to the Lord, and He gives us clear directives about how we should live in many situations. But God is well aware that it's our *heart beliefs* that drive us to behave in a particular manner.

People become addicted to alcohol or pornography because their minds are deceived and their consciences seared. Raging men and women hit their spouses or children because anger has overtaken their hearts and clouded their thought processes. People do what they do because of what's going on deep inside them. And what's going on inside them is what the Lord wants to cleanse, heal, and transform. He does not want some kind of robotic obedience to biblical statutes; He wants the passionate engagement and holy purity of our *hearts*.

That's why my goal is always to turn people back to their God and Savior, to encourage them to seek *His* direction. I believe—without a shadow of doubt—that He will speak clearly into the individual circumstances of every one of His beloved children. If His people genuinely ask for and desire guidance, I trust that God will reveal what's going on in their hearts, whether their decisions align with His. To do this, He may use a combination of Scripture, prayer, the counsel of others, or some other form of communication to make His will known. But He *will* do it. He will never abandon us to endlessly wonder what He would have us do.[2]

Is it possible, then, that a battered wife could pursue a legal dissolution to her marriage and be acting in God's will? Could the husband of a chemically or sexually addicted woman (even one who has not engaged in an extramarital affair) potentially separate from his wife in a godly way? Again, I do not believe in trying to apply strict "there are or are not biblical grounds for divorce" thinking to situations like these. What counts is what is in the heart of the person pursuing an end to the marriage. As 1 Samuel 16:7 declares, "The LORD doesn't make decisions the way you do! People judge by outward appearance, but the LORD looks at a person's thoughts and intentions" (NLT).

Asking what's at the heart of a person's desire for divorce or separation is vitally important. The sad reality is, some people want to end their marriages simply because they are "done" with a frustrating spouse, think they will be happier with someone else, or have "fallen out of love." In their book *Saving Your Marriage Before It Starts,* Drs. Les and Leslie Parrott claimed, "In marriage counseling, we hear again and again the sometimes plaintive, sometimes desperate words, 'I just don't love her anymore' or 'I love him, but I'm not in love with him.'"[3] What would you say to a couple like this?

Others want out of a miserable situation that seems to have no end in sight. These men and women must honestly answer a pointed and essential question asked by *The Marriage Masterpiece* author Al Janssen: "Is it worth fighting for an unhappy marriage?"[4] We've talked at length about the expectation that marriage will make us happy, that it will make us feel perpetually loved. But where does the rubber meet the road when it comes to our choice to stay committed?

Our very first decisions can shape the ultimate course of our marriage. Whether, for example, we enter in to and proceed in marriage with a God-centered view or a man-centered view determines the entire direction of our relationship. With a man-centered view, people stick with marriage only while their comforts, desires, and expectations are fulfilled. With a God-centered view, on the other hand, people preserve marriage because it brings glory to God and points a broken world to a redeeming, reconciling Savior.[5]

The rubber meets the road at the point where you pray, as Jesus did, "Not My will, but Yours be done" (Luke 22:42, NASB). In some instances, pursuing a legal end to your marriage may be His will. But selfishly choosing divorce is a "my will be done" decision. I needn't tell you whether or not this brings glory to God.

Even in light of this, however, allow me to say again: What ultimately matters is what's at the heart of your decision. I do not know your heart—no one else can know the intentions of your mind—but *God* does, and He will reveal His path for you. It's up to you whether to obey or rebel.

I'm not saying that it will be easy to choose His will over yours. In fact, I'm confident it may be rather difficult. I'm also not saying that there couldn't be nuances and complications that make it seem like divorce is the right option for you when it's actually not; there might be. But that does not make any choice outside of His will right. If you are not sure that *His* will is clear, the simple (though sometimes agonizingly difficult) solution is to wait. Trust Him to guide you and choose to obey—no matter what. His way is always best, both for you and for those around you.

Before you get married, it's crucial that you know—not merely in your head but with every fiber of your being—that God hates divorce (see Malachi 2:16). That wording might strike you as offensive or extreme, but I assure you, the Hebrew is far more intense. God hates divorce because it rips a hole in the picture of Christ and the church that He's painting through every couple. God hates seeing marriages dissolve because it's not His best for the children He loves.

It *is* worth fighting for an unhappy marriage because until heaven, every earthly story is unfinished. No; scratch that. Every earthly story is *gloriously* unfinished. What a gift it is that no matter what a couple has gone through, or is currently enduring, the Lord can still work redemption and hope, bringing new life from the ashes. No love is dead when it is offered into His hands.

Can He turn a frustrating marriage into a fruitful one? Yes. Can He help you fall in love again with a spouse in whom you've lost interest and hope? Absolutely! Can He heal addicted or abusive men and women, restoring faithful and loving relationships to them? Yes, yes, yes! Because individuals still have their own choices to make, your painful marriage may not resolve in the way you desire—a spouse who turns back to the Lord and a healthy relationship. But the question "Is God able?" can be answered definitively:

> O Sovereign LORD! You have made the heavens and earth by your great power. Nothing is too hard for you! You are loving and kind to thousands, though children suffer for their parents' sins. You are the great and powerful God, the LORD Almighty. You have all wisdom and do great and mighty miracles. You are very aware of the conduct of all people, and you reward them according to their deeds. (Jeremiah 32:17-19, NLT, emphasis added)

It's absolutely vital that we remember that God *is* able. It's also important that we know that in marriage, there is always a way out. And perhaps it will surprise you that the way out is *not* divorce. The way out in marriage, no matter how "out of love" a spouse feels, no matter how unhappy things have become, is to put everything back on the line for the Lord. And though putting everything in God's hands may not guarantee us a marriage that lasts forever, it does keep us in His will. We cannot control the decisions of others or the intentions of their hearts. But you and I can determine to live with our minds and wills open and obedient before Him.

As with the pain of rejection and abandonment, I hope with all my heart that you will not ever have to face the question, "Will I choose divorce?" But if you do, perhaps you will remember this chapter. By no means is this section intended as a comprehensive treatment on the issue (such is not the purpose of this book). I do pray, however, that your expectations about marriage lasting forever have been shaped by thinking about this issue as well as the other topics we've tackled. To continue your journey, turn with me now to some questions for meditation and further study.

Pressing On . . .

1. What did you think of my claim, "Standing at the altar, wide-eyed with the wonder of marriage, few people picture themselves facing a forced reentry into singlehood. . . . Since couples don't usually pass away simultaneously, [however,] a high percentage of married people will—at some point in their lives—become single again"? Is this a difficult reality for you to face? Why or why not?

2. Do you think most people—even most Christians—would describe the purpose of marriage with a God-centered view (marriage brings glory to God and directs a hurting world to its reconciling Redeemer) or a man-centered view (marriage should fulfill the needs, desires, and expectations of individuals, and if it does not, those individuals have the right to end the marriage)? What did you think of the differences between a God-centered view of marriage and a man-centered view of marriage that this chapter highlighted?

3. If you found yourself in a situation similar to Danielle's, would it have been difficult for you to wait on the Lord during the eight months of separation? Many people would have counseled Danielle

to divorce Dave on the grounds of "emotional infidelity," claiming he betrayed her trust by lying to her repeatedly. Danielle, however, felt that the Lord wanted her to wait. Eventually, after Dave's sexual indiscretion was uncovered, she did seek legal annulment. What do you think about this? How would you counsel someone in a comparable circumstance? How do you feel about the gray areas we discussed in the last section of this chapter? Would you counsel someone whose alcoholic spouse is completely uninterested in treatment or a perpetrator of domestic violence in the same way? Why or why not? What Scriptures would you use to back up your position?

4. We repeatedly noted in this chapter that God is faithful and true. You can use these verses from Psalm 89, an awesome proclamation of God's faithfulness, as a springboard for both discussion and meditation:

> *I will sing of the tender mercies of the LORD forever!*
> *Young and old will hear of your faithfulness.*
> *Your unfailing love will last forever.*
> *Your faithfulness is as enduring as the*
> *heavens.*
> *All heaven will praise your miracles, LORD;*
> *myriads of angels will praise you for your*
> *faithfulness.*
> *For who in all of heaven can compare with the LORD?*
> *What mightiest angel is anything like the LORD?*
> *The highest angelic powers stand in awe of God.*
> *He is far more awesome than those who*
> *surround his throne.*
> *O LORD God Almighty!*

Where is there anyone as mighty as you, LORD?
Faithfulness is your very character. (verses
1-2,5-8, NLT)

5. In a recent e-mail, Danielle wrote some words of encouragement for all of us who know people who have unexpectedly become single again. I'd like to close with her thoughts:

> *Please don't judge your sisters who are single again. You really*
> *don't know what you would do in any given situation until you*
> *walk in [it]. The way I counsel women in troubled marriages*
> *is different now that my marriage has ended. I still absolutely*
> *believe what the Word says about marriage and divorce . . . none*
> *of that has changed. But the way I handle the pain in wom-*
> *en's hearts has changed since I've walked through my own dark*
> *seasons.*

Living through a painful marriage and/or the end of a marriage (whether it was a difficult or wonderful one) is something that changes your life forever. Perhaps you can close this chapter by praying for greater understanding for your friends who've undergone or are enduring this challenge.

Benediction

OUR JOURNEY TOGETHER IS coming to an end. And over the last ten chapters, we've ventured through some rather challenging terrain. I pray you've been encouraged and invigorated, even when the climb has seemed steep.

In reading a book like this, it would be impossible to come to the end and remember everything you've taken in. I pray, then, that you would return to sections and reread them, allowing God to do the work of healing and transformation that He desires. I also pray that He will clearly direct you in applying the truths that have moved you. Every reader will experience this book—any book, really—in a unique way. Journeying with the Father through the ideas we've explored has been and will continue to be a process of unfolding discernment, with Him showing you exactly what to take away.

Perhaps, however, my writing this concerns rather than comforts you. Maybe you wonder if it will be difficult to figure out what particulars the Lord would have you work or meditate on further. Let me put your heart at rest: God *will* reveal to you what He wants, both from and for you—He's promised to do it! The following verses from Isaiah 42 offer a beautiful description of how the Lord will direct you:

> *I'll take the hand of those who don't know the way,*
> *who can't see where they're going.*
> *I'll be a personal guide to them,*
> *directing them through unknown country.*
> *I'll be right there to show them what roads to take,*
> *make sure they don't fall into the ditch.*
> *These are the things I'll be doing for them—*
> *sticking with them, not leaving them for a*
> *minute. (verse 16)*

God is a *personal* and *loving* guide for us. He walks with us through the unknown country. What hope this gives as we tackle subjects like singleness and marriage. Inevitably, with any discussion of relationships, we wade into the depths of our brokenness. But as we do, He promises to protect us, stick with us, make sure we are safe, whole, and fulfilled.

Throughout this book, we've acknowledged over and over again how tempting it is to look to another human to meet our needs, to validate our worth, to give us a sense of belonging. But we've also seen that what we so often look to a friend, family member, or spouse to provide, only God can. He truly is the Source of every good and perfect gift (see James 1:17). Everything your heart aches for in a spouse *can* be found in Jesus.

And I don't say that so you'll stop pursuing or enjoying marriage, hoping or preparing for it. Instead, I say this so that, on the deepest level, you can be free from the false expectations and assumptions we've explored. If you know (in that profoundly experiential way we've talked about) that God is who He says He is, you will not *need* to look to marriage or a life partner to fulfill you.

You will be able to accept, as a gift from God, any state in which you find yourself. Whether you are single or married, when God is at the center of your life, you can "feast on the abundance of [His] house, and . . . drink from the river of [His] delights. For with [Him] is the fountain of life; in [His] light we see light" (Psalm 36:8-9, NRSV).

With *Him* is the fountain of life; in *His* light we see light. The world would like us to believe that love and romance are the pinnacle experiences of life (others might try to convince you that sex is). But drinking from the river of *His* delights is true Life. We crave the abundance of *His* house but too often settle for the paltry meals dished out by lesser gods.

No longer! I urge you, my friends: Look to none other than God. Though the world and its daily grind may press in, let the eyes of your heart be illumined. The eternal world is more real and more significant than that which we see.

If you're in a devastatingly unhappy marriage; if you've been single year after year, pining for a mate; if you just don't know what in the world God is up to in your life—remember this: On the night He was betrayed, Jesus washed His disciples' feet. Peter, especially, found Christ's behavior shocking and disturbing. But Jesus told His trusted companion, "You do not know now what I am doing, but later you will understand" (John 13:7, NRSV).

In this life, it often happens that we just can't wrap our brains around what He's doing. We don't comprehend it, and sometimes we don't want to. We don't want to be a bridesmaid . . . again. We don't want to feel disillusioned and misunderstood in a broken marriage. We don't know why the person we love pays attention to everyone but us, why so many relationships are painful and confusing. We may never fully "get it" while here on earth, but our Lord *promises* that someday we will understand.

I want to leave you now with a benediction from the book of Hebrews. It is both my prayer and my heart's desire for you:

> *May God, who puts all things together,*
>   *makes all things whole,*
> *Who made a lasting mark through the sacrifice of Jesus . . .*
> *Put you together, provide you*
>   *with everything you need . . .*
> *Make [you] into what gives him most pleasure . . .*
> *All glory to Jesus forever and always! (13:20-21,*
>   *emphasis added)*

> *Amen.*

Notes

INTRODUCTION

1. Beverly and Thomas Alan Rodgers, *The Singlehood Phenomenon* (Colorado Springs, CO: NavPress, 2006), 9.
2. Les and Leslie Parrott, *Saving Your Marriage Before It Starts* (Grand Rapids, MI: Zondervan, 2006), 14.
3. H. Norman Wright, *Now That You're Engaged,* rev. ed. of *So You're Getting Married* (Ventura, CA: Regal, 2005), 101.
4. Bill and Pam Farrel, *Every Marriage Is a Fixer-Upper* (Eugene, OR: Harvest House, 2005), 11.
5. Dr. Larry Crabb, *The Marriage Builder* (Grand Rapids, MI: Zondervan, 1982), 12.
6. Author Gary Thomas explores this question in his excellent book *Sacred Marriage* (Grand Rapids, MI: Zondervan, 2000); see especially pages 23 and following.

7. You can find excellent additional information by mining the resources from which I've quoted.

CHAPTER 1: I'll Always Feel Loved

1. We hear of Zossima's wisdom and discernment from various sources in *The Brothers K*. Early on, readers discover that Aloysha—the youngest of the Brothers Karamazov—has been strongly influenced by Father Zossima. The elder "struck Aloysha by some special quality of his soul" (Fyodor Dostoyevsky, *The Brothers Karamazov,* trans. Richard Pevear and Larissa Volokhonsky (New York: Farrar, Straus & Giroux, 1990), 29. The narrator also reveals, "Many said of the elder Zossima that, having for so many years received all those who came to him to open their hearts, thirsting for advice and for a healing word, having taken into his soul so many confessions, sorrows, confidences, he acquired in the end such fine discernment that he could tell, from the first glance at a visiting stranger's face, what was in his mind, what he needed, and even what kind of suffering tormented his conscience" (also page 29). And even the wicked and drunken patriach of the Karamazov family calls Zossima "the most honest man there [in the monastery]" (page 23).

2. Fyodor Dostoyevsky, *The Brothers Karamazov,* trans. Constance Garnett, ed. John Bayley, 11th printing ed. (New York: Signet Classics, 1999), 48.

3. Dean Brackley, *The Call to Discernment in Troubled Times* (New York: Crossroad, 2004), 10.

4. Paul Chance, "The Trouble with Love," *Psychology Today* (February 1988): 44–47.

5. Beverly and Thomas Alan Rodgers, *The Singlehood Phenomenon* (Colorado Springs, CO: NavPress, 2006), 121.

6. Rodgers and Rodgers, 121–122.

7. Rodgers and Rodgers, 119.

8. Rodgers and Rodgers, 122.

9. Rodgers and Rodgers, 122.

10. In the NRSV, Paul used this phrase ten times in the book of Romans (see 3:4,6,31; 6:2,15; 7:7,13; 9:14; and 11:1,11).

11. Although the original quote was taken from Viorst's public speaking, a very similar quote can be found in Judith Viorst, *Grown-Up Marriage* (New York: Simon & Schuster, 2003), 1: "In a grown-up marriage we recognize that we don't always have to be in love with each other. In fact, we are well aware that we couldn't possibly always be in love with each other. But *a grown-up marriage enables us, when we fall out of love with each other, to stick around until we fall back in*" (emphasis added).

12. Anne Morrow Lindbergh, *Gift from the Sea* (New York: Pantheon Books, 1986), 108.

13. Mike Mason, *The Mystery of Marriage* (Sisters, OR: Multnomah, 1985), 25.

14. See Mason, 22–25.

15. See Mason, 27.

16. See Mason, 21.

17. Eliza Tabor, *St. Olave's: A Novel* (New York: HarperCollins, 1864 edition), 112, digitized January 24, 2007, and available on google.com/books.

18. Les and Leslie Parrott, *Saving Your Marriage Before It Starts* (Grand Rapids, MI: Zondervan, 2006), 27.

CHAPTER 2: I'll Feel Whole, Complete, and Satisfied

1. Gary Thomas, *Sacred Marriage* (Grand Rapids, MI: Zondervan, 2000), 83.

2. Dan B. Allender and Tremper Longman III, *Intimate Allies* (Wheaton, IL: Tyndale, 1995), 146.

3. Anais Nin, *The Diary of Anais Nin: Vol. 1 (1931–1934)* (New York: Harvest Books, 1994), 244, quoted in Les and Leslie Parrott, *Saving Your Marriage Before It Starts* (Grand Rapids, MI: Zondervan, 2006), 19.

4. Rabbi Joshua Loth Liebman, *Hope for Man* (New York: Simon & Schuster, 1966), quoted in Les and Leslie Parrott, *Saving Your Marriage Before It Starts,* 20.

5. C. S. Lewis, *George MacDonald* (New York: Macmillan, 1954), 16–17.

6. Robert McKee, *Story: Substance, Structure, Style, and the Principles of Screenwriting* (New York: HarperCollins, 1997), 5. I was referred to McKee by John Eldredge, who quoted him in the book *Epic* (Nashville: Thomas Nelson, 2007), 5.

7. Simone Weil, *Waiting for God* (New York: Harper Perennial Modern Classics, 2001), xxxi, 138.

8. Nicole Johnson, *Keeping a Princess Heart in a Not-So-Fairy-Tale World* (Nashville: Thomas Nelson, 2003), 65.

CHAPTER 3: **I Won't Feel Lonely Anymore**

1. "That's What the Lonely Is For" by David Wilcox, © 1994 Irving Music, Inc., Midnight Ocean Bonfire Music, All Rights Administered by Irving Music, Inc. (BMI). Used by Permission. All Rights Reserved.

2. Tim Hansel, *Through the Wilderness of Loneliness* (Elgin, IL: LifeJourney Books, 1991), 162–164.

3. Hansel, 141–142.

4. There are times when we feel incredibly lonely, even though people around us may be reaching out. Sin, shame, pain, or uncontrollable life circumstances may cause you to feel desperately lonely, even when options for connection and community are present. This I would call a "perceived" season of

loneliness. An actual season of loneliness occurs when there are few or no chances for connecting with others—for instance, after you've moved, transferred jobs, changed churches, or had a falling-out with friends. Whether your loneliness is perceived or actual, it often *feels* the same, and God uses both perceived and actual loneliness to shape us.

5. For an excellent discussion of this, see Hansel, 107. Quote from page 110, emphasis added.

6. Henri Nouwen, *Reaching Out* (New York: Image Books, 1986), 34.

7. For an excellent discussion of this, see Hansel, 159.

8. Nouwen, 49–50.

9. For an easy-to-use personality test and abridged explanation of the Myers-Briggs method, see David Keirsey and Marilyn Bates, *Please Understand Me*, 3rd ed. (Del Mar, CA: Prometheus Nemesis Book Company, 1984). For a spiritual perspective on temperament and some prayer exercises to help you explore your own personality, see Chester P. Michael and Marie C. Norrisey, *Prayer and Temperament* (Charlottesville, VA: Open Door, 1991).

10. Carol Bainbridge, "Gifted Children . . . 'Extrovert,'" http://giftedkids.about.com/od/glossary/g/extrovert.htm (accessed January 3, 2008).

11. Dr. Emerson Eggerichs, *Love and Respect* (Nashville: Thomas Nelson, 2004), 127–128.

12. See Eggerichs, 127–129.

CHAPTER 4: **Life Will Be So Much Better**

1. *The Princess Bride*, VHS, directed by Rob Reiner, screenplay by William Goldman (Los Angeles: 20th Century-Fox Film Corp., 1987).

2. John Levy and Ruth Munroe, *The Happy Family* (New York:

Knopf, 1959), emphasis added.

3. Mike Mason, *The Mystery of Marriage* (Sisters, OR: Multnomah, 1985), 165, 170–171.

4. Dennis and Barbara Rainey, *Starting Your Marriage Right* (Wheaton, IL: Tyndale, 2000), 7.

5. Rainey and Rainey, 8–9.

6. Otto Piper, *The Biblical View of Sex and Marriage* (New York: Scribner, 1960), 153.

CHAPTER 5: **I Won't Have to Worry About Money**

1. See Gary Thomas, *Sacred Marriage* (Grand Rapids, MI: Zondervan, 2000), 136.

2. See Randy Alcorn, *Money, Possessions, and Eternity* (Wheaton, IL: Tyndale, 1989), 16–17.

3. Alcorn, 18, 21.

4. Alcorn, 414.

5. Ian R. McGreal, ed., *Great Thinkers of the Western World* (New York: HarperCollins, 1992), 187–190.

6. Of course, we need to be careful with this promise. This does not mean that if you have lived irresponsibly and failed to pay your electric bill, God will supernaturally sustain your lights and entertainment center. The consequences of foolish financial decisions may hurt us; they can also, however, turn us back to the Lord and to His people, who can help us spend, save, and give in a wiser manner. The penalties for *other people's* silly choices may impinge on our comfort and care as well. We must never assume responsibility for the mistakes of others, but we are sometimes forced to share in the undesirable consequences of their actions. If you are in this unfortunate situation, I encourage you to pursue financial counseling. Perhaps a member of your church is a certified financial planner, someone who could help get you

(and your loved one) back on track. I urge you to pray and look for God's provision in this time of need. The promise that "the Lord will provide" may not always mean a mysterious check in your mailbox, but because we can trust in His promises, we *know* that God will make good on His word. He will protect and preserve us.

7. See Alcorn, 310.

8. See H. Norman Wright, *Now That You're Engaged,* rev. ed. of *So You're Getting Married* (Ventura, CA: Regal, 2005), 68–69.

9. I most highly recommend Randy Alcorn's book *Money, Possessions, and Eternity* (though I have quoted from my copy, the 1989 edition, Tyndale released an updated and revised edition in 2003). Richard Foster's *Money, Sex, and Power* (San Francisco: HarperCollins, 1985) may be a bit out-of-date as far as terms and tips, but the *principles* are biblical, clear, and essential. For outstanding biblical counsel, as well as a list of many practical resources, refer to Crown Financial Ministries (CFM) at http://www.crown.org. Howard Dayton, cofounder of CFM, has also published two excellent books: *Your Money Counts* (Wheaton, IL: Tyndale, 1997) and *Your Money Map* (Chicago: Moody, 2006). NavPress also has an excellent book and workbook by Matt Bell titled *Money, Purpose, Joy: The Proven Path to Uncommon Financial Success* (Colorado Springs, CO: 2008).

10. See Alcorn, 319.

11. See U.S. Department of Labor *News,* May 9, 2007, http://www .bls.gov/news.release/archives/famee_05092007.pdf.

12. Alcorn, 315, 317.

13. A. W. Tozer, *The Pursuit of God* (Harrisburg, PA: Christian Publications, 1958), 21–22.

CHAPTER 6: I'll Know What to Do with the Rest of My Life

1. Anne Frank, *Anne Frank: The Diary of a Young Girl,* trans. B. M. Mooyaart (New York: Bantam Books, 1993), entry February 12, 1944, ver. A.
2. Les and Leslie Parrott, *Saving Your Marriage Before It Starts* (Grand Rapids, MI: Zondervan, 2006), 139.
3. Nicole Johnson, *Keeping a Princess Heart in a Not-So-Fairy-Tale World* (Nashville: Thomas Nelson, 2003), 173.
4. Paulo Coelho, *Veronika Decides to Die,* trans. Margaret Jull Costa (New York: Harper Perennial, 2001), 106.
5. Rick Warren, *The Purpose-Driven Life* (Grand Rapids, MI: Zondervan, 2002), 17.
6. The Westminster Shorter Catechism AD 1647, accessed through Quick Verse v. 8.0, copyright Findex.com, Inc., 2004.
7. Johnson, 174–175.

CHAPTER 7: Sex Won't Be an Issue Anymore

1. You can find *Intimate Issues* (Colorado Springs, CO: WaterBrook, 1999), *Gift-Wrapped by God* (Colorado Springs, CO: Water-Brook, 2002), and *Intimacy Ignited* (Colorado Springs, CO: NavPress, 2004) at your local bookstore or online. Any would be an excellent source for further information and deeper study, but if you are a younger single, *Gift-Wrapped by God* is probably the best place to start. *Intimate Issues* and *Intimacy Ignited* detail some issues of sexuality that will most benefit older singles or engaged and married couples.
2. For a great exploration of some of the reasons God created sex, see Lorraine Pintus and Linda Dillow, *Gift-Wrapped by God* (Colorado Springs, CO: WaterBrook, 2002), 18–22.
3. Gary Thomas, *Sacred Marriage* (Grand Rapids, MI: Zondervan, 2000), 196.

4. Mike Mason, *The Mystery of Marriage* (Sisters, OR: Multnomah, 1985), 153.
5. Stephen Arterburn and Fred Stoeker, with Mike Yorkey, *Every Man's Battle* (Colorado Springs, CO: WaterBrook, 2000), 63–64.
6. Please refer to my books *Every Thought Captive* (Colorado Springs, CO: NavPress, 2006), 125–152 and *The Life You Crave* (Colorado Springs, CO: NavPress, 2008), 90–98 if you are interested in reading more.

CHAPTER 8: I'll Feel Pretty (and Witty and Bright)

1. Forgive me. Once upon a time, I worked as a choreographer for our college's production of *West Side Story*. I just couldn't resist this obvious reference.
2. In previous books, such as *Every Thought Captive* (Colorado Springs, CO: NavPress, 2006) and *The Life You Crave* (Colorado Springs, CO: NavPress, 2008), I talk more about my personal struggle with body-image issues as well as what God thinks about our bodies, beauty, and how we handle our physical appearance.
3. Adapted from Jerusha Clark, *Every Thought Captive*, 162–163.
4. C. S. Lewis, *The Screwtape Letters* (New York: Macmillan, 1951), 102–103.
5. See Nicole Johnson, *Keeping a Princess Heart in a Not-So-Fairy-Tale World* (Nashville: Thomas Nelson, 2003), 119, for an excellent discussion of this.
6. William Gurnall, *The Christian in Complete Armour,* ed. James S. Bell Jr. (1655; Lindale, TX: World Challenge, 1994), 11.
7. James D. and Evelyn Eaton Whitehead, *A Sense of Sexuality: Christian Love and Intimacy* (New York: Doubleday, 1989), 75.
8. If you struggle with the words "gentle and quiet spirit," allow me to suggest that you find a good commentary on 1 Peter and read

what these words actually mean. When I discovered a "gentle and quiet spirit" was not a personality style but rather the position of a heart surrendered to God and still before Him (which may be true of even the most vivacious and dramatic women), I was much relieved.

9. Margery Williams, *The Velveteen Rabbit* (New York: Doubleday, 1991), 8.

CHAPTER 9: I'll Have a Happy Family

1. Les and Leslie Parrott, *Saving Your Marriage Before It Starts* (Grand Rapids, MI: Zondervan, 2006), 23.

2. Dan B. Allender and Tremper Longman III, *Intimate Allies* (Wheaton, IL: Tyndale, 1995), 218.

3. H. Norman Wright, *Now That You're Engaged*, rev. ed. of *So You're Getting Married* (Ventura, CA: Regal, 2005), 106.

4. A special and loving thanks to Louie Moesta, who pointed out this excellent biblical example to me. Love you, K. S.!

5. Douglas Weiss, *The Ten-Minute Marriage Principle* (New York: FaithWords, 2007), 139.

6. Lewis B. Smedes, *The Art of Forgiving* (New York: Ballantine Books, 1996), 59. I also highly recommend Smedes' book *Forgive and Forget* (New York: HarperSanFrancisco, 1997).

7. For more, see my books *Every Thought Captive* (Colorado Springs, CO: NavPress, 2006), 87–105 and *The Life You Crave* (Colorado Springs, CO: NavPress, 2008), 175–179. Both include lengthier sections on forgiveness.

8. Wright, 139.

9. See Parrott and Parrott, 89–90.

CHAPTER 10: **It Will Be Forever**

1. On the subject of grief, you may consider Doug Manning's book *Don't Take My Grief Away from Me* (Oklahoma City, OK: In-Sight Books, 2005) or C. S. Lewis's classic *A Grief Observed* (New York: HarperCollins, 1961). The website GriefShare.org gives helpful information and lists numerous resources that may help with the process of grieving. Bill Dunn and Kathy Leonard's *Through a Season of Grief* (Nashville: Thomas Nelson, 2004), a GriefShare devotional, is devoted to those who are mourning a loss. This 365-day devotional ministers beyond the initial shock and into the coming year of bereavement. Full of biblical comfort and sound advice, the book features insights from well-known and respected Christian leaders such as Kay Arthur, Larry Crabb, and Jack Hayford. On the subjects of divorce and separation, Dr. Les Carter's book *Grace and Divorce* (San Francisco: Jossey-Bass, 2004) can be helpful, as can Jeenie Gordon's *Cementing the Torn Strands: Rebuilding Your Life After Divorce* (Grand Rapids, MI: Revell, 1991). The website DivorceCare.org also provides excellent help for hurting people and those who love them.

2. If you struggle with knowing God's will for your circumstances or your life in general, allow me to refer you to my book *The Life You Crave: The Promise of Discernment* (Colorado Springs, CO: NavPress, 2008). In this work, I help people develop their capacity to make wise decisions based on God's clear direction. Discernment is a gift of the Holy Spirit, available to *all* believers. Sadly, though Christians often speak of having a personal relationship with God, many fail to cultivate the "personal" dynamic of their intimacy with the Lord. God promises to communicate with us directly, specifically, and *person-to-person* (see 1 Corinthians 2:5-16). To live well and make wise choices, discernment

is something we all need. In many ways, it has become a lost art; however, it doesn't have to remain that way.

3. Les and Leslie Parrott, *Saving Your Marriage Before It Starts* (Grand Rapids, MI: Zondervan, 2006), 40.

4. Al Janssen asks this question in his book *The Marriage Master-piece* (Wheaton, IL: Tyndale, 2001), 9.

5. See Gary Thomas, *Sacred Marriage* (Grand Rapids, MI: Zondervan, 2000), 32; in this section Thomas quoted C. J. Mahaney's audiotape series on marriage titled *According to Plan*.

About the Author

JERUSHA CLARK is the author of *Every Thought Captive*, *The Life You Crave*, and *Inside a Cutter's Mind* and the coauthor of four other books, including the best seller *I Gave Dating a Chance*. She's passionate about ministering to people and wrestling with the questions closest to their hearts. Jerusha resides in Escondido, California, with her husband, Jeramy, a pastor at Emmanuel Faith Community Church, and her daughters, Jocelyn and Jasmine.

More great titles from Jerusha Clark!

Every Thought Captive
Jerusha Clark
978-1-57683-868-6

Every Thought Captive explores the deepest recesses of the feminine mind and examines the sources of our insecurities, unholy desires, and anxieties. Drawing from her own experiences as well as other women's, best-selling author Jerusha Clark shares insights from God's Word that provide a road map to victory over toxic beliefs.

The Life You Crave
Jerusha Clark
978-1-60006-055-7

Find out how practicing biblical discernment enables us to live well. Using research, the riches of God's Word, and the personal experiences of many, Jerusha Clark helps us discover the power of choosing well. Turn the promise of an abundant life into reality and start living the life you crave.

Inside a Cutter's Mind
Jerusha Clark with Dr. Earl Henslin
978-1-60006-054-0

This book explores the complex problem of cutting, which has no easy solution. With an empathetic heart and a compassionate voice, Jerusha Clark brings light to a dark condition and delivers hope to victims and their loved ones.

To order copies, call NavPress at 1-800-366-7788
or log on to www.navpress.com.

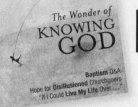